The Second Treatise of Civil Government

The Second Treatise of Civil Government

John Locke

Edited by Andrew Bailey

This edition is adapted from
The Broadview Anthology of Social and Political Thought;

General Editors:
Andrew Bailey
Samantha Brennan
Will Kymlicka
Jacob Levy
Alex Sager
Clark Wolf

broadview press

Library and Archives Canada Cataloguing in Publication

Locke, John, 1632-1704
[Essay concerning the true original, extent and end of civil government]
   The second treatise of civil government / John Locke ; edited by Andrew Bailey.

"This edition is adapted from The Broadview Anthology of Social and Political
   Thought; general editors: Andrew Bailey, Samantha Brennan, Will Kymlicka,
   Jacob Levy, Alex Sager, Clark Wolf."
Originally published under title: Essay concerning the true original, extent and end
   of civil government.
Includes bibliographical references and index.
ISBN 978-1-55481-156-4 (paperback)

   1. Political science—Early works to 1800. 2. Toleration—Early works to 1800.
3. Liberty—Early works to 1800. I. Bailey, Andrew, 1969-, editor II. Title.
III. Title: Essay concerning the true original, extent and end of civil government

JC153.L85 2015   320.01   C2015-903239-3

Broadview Press is an independent, international publishing house, incorporated in 1985.

We welcome comments and suggestions regarding any aspect of our publications—please feel free to contact us at the addresses below or at broadview@broadviewpress.com.

North America
PO Box 1243, Peterborough, Ontario K9J 7H5, Canada
555 Riverwalk Parkway, Tonawanda, NY 14150, USA
Tel: (705) 743-8990; Fax: (705) 743-8353
email: customerservice@broadviewpress.com

UK, Europe, Central Asia, Middle East, Africa, India, and Southeast Asia
Eurospan Group, 3 Henrietta St., London WC2E 8LU, United Kingdom
Tel: 44 (0) 1767 604972; Fax: 44 (0) 1767 601640
email: eurospan@turpin-distribution.com

Australia and New Zealand
Footprint Books
1/6a Prosperity Parade, Warriewood, NSW 2102, Australia
Tel: + 61 2 9997 3973; Fax: + 61 2 9997 3185
email: info@footprint.com.au

www.broadviewpress.com

Copy-edited by Robert M. Martin

Broadview Press acknowledges the financial support of the Government of Canada for our publishing activities. **Canadä**

Typesetting and assembly: True to Type Inc., Claremont, Canada.

PRINTED IN CANADA

Contents

Portrait of John Locke by Sir Godfrey Kneller, 1697.

Introduction

Who Was John Locke?

John Locke was born in the Somerset countryside, near the town of Bristol, in 1632. His parents were small landowners—minor gentry—who raised the young Locke according to strict Protestant principles. Thanks to the influence of one of his father's friends, Locke was able to gain a place at Westminster School, at the time the best school in England, where he studied Greek, Latin, and Hebrew. He went on to Christ Church College, Oxford, and graduated with a BA in 1656. Shortly afterwards he was made a Senior Student of his college—a kind of teaching position; he would remain at the college until 1684, when the king of England, Charles II, personally (and illegally) demanded his expulsion.

During the 1650s and early 1660s Locke lectured on Greek and rhetoric at Oxford; but he was idle and unhappy, and became increasingly bored by the traditional philosophy of his day. He developed an interest in medicine and physical science (in 1675 he tried and failed to gain the degree of Doctor of Medicine), and in 1665 Locke left the confines of the academic world, and began to make his way into the world of politics and science. In the winter of 1665-66 he was ambassador to the German state of Brandenburg, where his first-hand observation of religious toleration between Calvinists, Lutherans, Catholics, and Anabaptists made a big impression on him.

A chance encounter in 1666 was the decisive turning-point in Locke's life: he met a nobleman called Lord Ashley, who was then the Chancellor of the Exchequer, and soon went to live at Ashley's London house as his confidant and medical adviser. In 1668, Locke was responsible for a life-saving surgical operation on Ashley, implanting a small silver spigot to drain off fluid from a cyst on his liver; the lord never forgot his gratitude, and wore the small tap in his side for the rest of his life. Under Ashley's patronage, Locke had both the leisure to spend several years working on his *Essay Concerning Human Understanding*, and a sequence of lucrative and interesting government positions, including one in which he was part of a group drafting the constitution of the new colony of Carolina in the Americas.

Ashley's support was also essential in giving Locke—an introverted and hyper-sensitive soul, who suffered for most of his life from bad asthma and generally poor health—the confidence to do original philosophy. Locke never married, was a life-long celibate, and shied away from drinking parties and a hectic social life, but he enjoyed the attentions of lady admirers and throughout his life had many loyal friends and got on especially well with some of his friends' children.

Locke spent the years from 1675 to 1679 traveling in France (where he expected to die of tuberculosis, but survived—he spent a large portion of his life confidently expecting an early death), and when he returned to England it was to a very unsettled political situation. The heir to the British throne, Charles II's younger brother James, was a Catholic, and his succession was feared by many politicians, including Ashley—who by this time was now the Earl of Shaftesbury—and his political party, the Whigs. Their greatest worry was that the return of a Catholic monarchy would mean the return of religious oppression to England, as was happening in parts of Europe. Charles, however, stood by his brother and in 1681 Shaftesbury was sent to prison in the Tower of London on a charge of high treason. Shaftesbury was acquitted by a grand jury, but he fled to Holland and died a few months later (spending his last few hours, the story goes, discussing a draft of Locke's *Essay* with his friends). Locke, in danger as a known associate of Shaftesbury's, followed his example in 1683 and secretly moved to the Netherlands, where he had to spend a year underground evading arrest by Dutch government agents acting on King Charles's behalf. While in Holland he re-wrote material for the *Essay*, and molded it towards its final state. It immediately attracted international attention following publication of an abridged version in a French scholarly periodical.

James's brief reign as James II ended in 1688, with the accession of his Protestant daughter Mary and her husband William of Orange. The political tumult in England had subsided enough for Locke to return, and he moved as a permanent house-guest to an estate called Oates about 25 miles from London. He returned to political life (though he refused the post of ambassador to Brandenburg, on the grounds of his ill health), and played a significant role in the loosening of restrictions on publishers and authors.

In 1689, when Locke was 57, the results of his 30 years of thinking and writing were suddenly published in a flood. First, published anonymously, came the *Letter Concerning Toleration*, and shortly thereafter, also anonymously, *Two Treatises on Government*. Finally, *An Essay Concerning Human Understanding* was published under Locke's own name, to almost instant acclaim.

By now one of the most famous men in England, Locke continued to write and publish until his death fifteen years later. Among his many publications were one on the proper control of the currency for the English government; *Some Thoughts Concerning Education* (which, apparently, was historically important in shaping the toilet-training practices of the English educated classes); a work on the proper care and cultivation of fruit trees; and a careful commentary on the Epistles of St. Paul. He died quietly, reading in his study, in October 1704.

What Was Locke's Overall Philosophical Project?

Locke and British Empiricism

The focus of this volume is on Locke's political writing, but it is helpful by way of background to also be aware of his importance in another area of philosophy: Locke was a major figure in the school of thought nowadays called "British empiricism." In the view of Locke and other empiricists of his time, we are born with a mind like a blank sheet of paper—in Latin, a *tabula rasa*—without any innate knowledge, but with certain natural powers. We use these powers to adapt ourselves to the social and physical environment into which we are born. Two especially important natural powers are the capacity for conscious sense experience and the capacity to feel pleasure and pain, and it is from the interaction of these capacities with the environment that we acquire all of our ideas, knowledge, and habits of mind. All meaningful language must be connected to the ideas that we thus acquire; to use words without correspondence to such ideas is an abuse of language and a serious source of intellectual errors—errors which can have harmful consequences for social and moral life, as well as for the growth of the sciences.

An Essay Concerning Human Understanding was Locke's attempt to present a systematic and detailed empiricist account of the human mind and human knowledge. It also includes an account of the nature of language, and touches on philosophical issues to do with logic, religion, metaphysics, and ethics. Locke was optimistic about the potential of human beings to come to know the world; above all, he believed our human capacities to be sufficient to produce certain knowledge of the existence of things in the world corresponding to our basic sense-perceptions. Locke was also confident of humans' capacity (through the power of reason, rather than of sense perception) to achieve sure knowledge of the existence of God, and of moral principles. But he also believed there to be some things human beings cannot ever come to know with certainty—for example, some areas of religious doctrine and scientific theory. In these cases the best we can do is to make skillful guesses. God has given us the capacity to effectively get by in the world by making these careful guesses, according to Locke, but he has not given us the capacity to know for sure whether or not our guesses are correct. (This is one reason why Locke believed we should be tolerant of other people's religious beliefs.)

Locke's Political Philosophy

A central theme uniting all of Locke's work is anti-authoritarianism. This manifests itself in his advocacy of reasoning and sense-perception, rather than authority, as the only reliable ways to get knowledge, and in his insistence that these faculties be used to determine what political and social institutions would contribute best to human flourishing. His major political works are the *Two Treatises of Government* (with the *Second Treatise* generally acknowledged to be much more important than the *First*). In this work he argues at length against the divine right of kings, and the idea that people are naturally subject to a monarch; instead, he claims, we are naturally free and equal, possessing natural rights—that is, rights that exist independent of any society's arrangements—to "life, liberty, and property." The restrictions imposed by government are legitimate only when we agree to give up the liberty we would have in the "state of nature" for the sake of the stability and order government may provide; but when a government fails to provide for the public good, it can legitimately be replaced, since it exists only by the agreement of the governed. He considers at length what sorts of arrangements for government might best suit the purposes and constraints he urges. His prescription incorporates many of the elements of contemporary liberal democracy. Locke's work is also important for the views it expresses on religious toleration—again providing in outline what has become a central principle of the modern liberal state.

He was, in sum, a very early defender of what we have now come to recognize as typically modern values. He advocated abandoning uncritical acceptance of Greek and Roman history, literature and philosophy, and of Christian theology, championing independent thought, secular values, and the power of modern ideas and rationally guided social change.

What Is the Structure of *The Second Treatise*?

Locke's *Two Treatises* were originally published together, though their focuses are somewhat different. *The First Treatise of Government* contains an extended attack on the idea of a divinely ordained, hereditary, absolute monarchy, concentrating on the arguments of an influential advocate, Sir Robert Filmer. Locke ridicules Filmer's attempt to prove the divine right of kings on the basis of the claim that God gave sovereignty to Adam, and that this would pass to future kings as Adam's descendants. Some commentators have remarked that Filmer's arguments hardly justify such distinguished and extended philosophical consideration; Locke himself seems at points a bit apologetic about this, remarking, in effect, that this was the best presentation he could find of a foolish position.

In the *Second Treatise*, Locke begins with the idea, no doubt derived from the thought of Thomas Hobbes, that to justify the existence of government we need to think about the state of nature—that is, about what human social arrangements would be like without government. This state would be anarchy, lacking any written law or enforcement, but, contrary to Hobbes, Locke thought that it would not be lawless: the moral law, provided by God and discoverable by reason ("writ in the hearts of all mankind"), would still bind humans. This law tells us, for example, that all men[1] should be treated as equals—that no one has the right to dominate or enslave another—and that "no one ought to harm another in his life, health, liberty, or possessions." So the state of nature would not necessarily be a Hobbesian state of constant warfare of each against all, and could, at least in principle, be peaceful.

In Chapter 5, Locke attempts to derive the right of property from his considerations about natural moral law. One naturally owns one's own body, and one also legitimately owns unowned things that one "mixes his labor" with. But this is true only provided (the famous "Lockean proviso") that one does not take more than one needs, and that one leaves enough, and as good, for others. Locke is sometimes taken in this chapter to have set out ideas that facilitated the emergence of modern capitalism in the following century.

---

1   As with any seventeenth-century text, it is important to be wary about reading "men" inclusively as "human beings." Arguably, though, Locke was somewhat ahead of his time of these issues. Certainly he rejects the then-common view of women as property, but his views (as set out, for example, in Chapters 2 and 4 of the *First Treatise*, and in Chapter 6 of the *Second Treatise*) concerning the extent to which or the circumstances in which women might or might not be considered to have rights equal to those of men are not always clear or consistent.

In Chapter 7 and subsequent chapters, Locke gives what turns out to be, after all, a rather Hobbesian justification for society. In the state of nature, it would be up to each person to discover, interpret, and enforce these natural laws, and doing this is (at best) inconvenient; because people often differ in moral opinion, or are too weak to punish moral infringements, or are simply morally indifferent, this peace would be insecure. Our possessions would be threatened with theft, and our persons with violence. Although obligated by natural law to be peaceful, we would be likely to relapse into Hobbesian general warfare—as we do even in our days, whenever society collapses into anarchy. We would, then, voluntarily be willing to give up some of the freedom we enjoyed in the state of nature in exchange for governmental control of our actions—to transfer the right of enforcement of the law of nature to a civil government, "for the mutual preservation of their lives, liberties and estates, which I call by the general name, property." Interestingly, unlike most political contractarians, he appears to have believed that the state of nature and the contract to form society were both historically real—though so long ago that records have been lost.

Locke is careful to distance himself from Hobbes's conclusion that the contract justifies dominance by an absolute ruler; according to Locke, a tyrannical sovereign (in extreme cases) puts himself in a state of war with the people (in effect, a breach of the social contract)—in the event of which the people may legitimately revolt.

Some Useful Background Information

In the volatile world of the 1680s, setting out controversial political theories in print could be dangerous business. The climate in 1689 may have allowed for more freedom of expression than had been allowed for earlier in the decade, but we should not imagine there to have been freedom of expression in anything like the sense we think of it in modern, democratic societies. It is thus not surprising that the *Treatises* were published anonymously. And it is certainly conceivable that even those who published anonymously might, in those days, feel themselves to be constrained to say less than they would have liked to say— or to say some things they did not mean. For these reasons it is safer to speak of what the texts themselves say rather than of what Locke himself believed.

Though 1690 was the date printed on the title page of the first edition of the *Two Treatises*, it was in fact published in December of 1689.

Both the first and the second edition contained numerous errors; the text included here (as in most modern editions) is that of the third edition (1698), and includes corrections that Locke made on his copy of that edition but that he was not able to see incorporated into a planned fourth edition.

Capitalization and spelling have been modernized in the present edition, but Locke's seventeenth-century English may nevertheless be a bit daunting to readers. Sentences are very long, with subsidiary parts set off in commas. Many words and references need explanation to modern readers; this is provided in a large number of footnotes. Following is a list of a few important terms that Locke uses often, but with special meanings that may be somewhat unfamiliar:

arbitrary: When Locke speaks of an "arbitrary will" this does not mean just a whim or a random decision without reason. In his day, this meant simply something that one decides—that depends on someone's choice.

commonwealth. In Locke's day, this word had recently come to suggest a democracy or republican state, an association it still has. But Locke makes it clear in § 133 that he is using the word (in an older sense) to refer to any form of state or community.

enjoyment, enjoy: These words in Locke's usage do not imply taking delight in something, but merely making use of it, taking benefit from it.

moment: This word is frequently used to mean *importance*, as in "of great moment".

positive: This can mean explicit; a *positive law*, then, is one that is explicitly written down and passed by a legislative authority; this is contrasted, in Locke's view, with a *natural law*, which is inscribed in no law books, and applies to humans just because of human nature. A *positive agreement* is one explicitly stated and agreed upon; the contrast here is with a tacit (wordless) agreement that is just implied by actions and circumstances. *Positively* can also mean *clearly*.

presently: In Locke's day, this word was sometimes used to mean *immediately*, sometimes *soon*, and sometimes *at this (or that) time*. It is not always clear which meaning Locke intended in each of the many instances of this word.

prince: Like Machiavelli, Locke uses this term to refer to any ruler. (It does not have the sense more familiar nowadays: *son of the monarch*.)

Property

A key element of Locke's *Second Treatise* is its treatment in Chapter 5 of questions relating to property. The issues he discusses there, as to how a right to property may arise, are couched in ways that make them seem distant from late seventeenth-century England either in time ("Adam and ... Noah, and his sons") or in space ("several nations of the Americans"). But in fact they were issues very close to home. Central to the historical background here is the practice known in England as enclosure, whereby common land was appropriated (or "enclosed") by the landed gentry or others in positions of power. The intended result was a more efficient and profitable use of land for the landholders. The by-product was typically that peasants or tenant farmers and their families were displaced—sometimes with compensation, sometimes not—and forced to live elsewhere, often becoming destitute city dwellers. Enclosures are recorded in Britain as early as the twelfth century, but did not become common until the fifteenth century. Over the next four centuries the English landscape was transformed, and the medieval manorial system (in which commoners were granted access to common areas both for planting crops and for pasture) gave way to a system based on individual title to property. Until well into the seventeenth century enclosures were driven largely by the desire of land holders to profit from sheep farming. It was often more lucrative for the gentry to expel the commoners who had farmed their land (and paid rent, whether in cash or in crops), to enclose the land as private property, and then to turn it over to the farming of sheep; the price of wool rose sharply over these centuries. Around 1650 the price of wool leveled off. From then until the 1830s the practice of enclosure continued, but more commonly involved turning over the land appropriated from tenant farmers to larger scale farming of crops. Either way, enclosure remained controversial, often setting landlords not only against the peasantry but also against the monarchy. (A succession of monarchs opposed enclosures on the grounds both that they tended to bring down tax revenues and that they brought about increased vagrancy. It was not until the late seventeenth century—Locke's day— that a settled alliance of Parliamentarians and landlords in support of enclosures arose.)

What did it mean to "own" land in the seventeenth century? The law as to what constituted ownership remained largely undeveloped. Commoners, understandably enough, believed that they should have the right to continue to use land which was controlled by the lord or head of the manor but that had been shared communally since before anyone could remember. At the other end of the spectrum, writers such as Robert Filmer maintained a "patriarchalist" view: just as a father could take away the things that his children had been allowed to use, property could be taken away by a monarch (or by God); so no property "right" could be more than provisional.

There can be no doubt that Locke was concerned to establish the property rights of landowners against the claims of monarchists such as Filmer, but it is less obvious how he meant his arguments to apply to the disputes between landowners and commoners over the issues raised by enclosure—the great property rights controversy of the era. Locke frequently contrasts two sorts of people making claims to property: those, on the one hand, whose claim rests on the "improvement of labor" they have provided to the property, and those, on the other, who may have occupied the land but have not made it more productive through their labor. We might naturally think of "labor" as the physical work of the occupying tenants and not as the acts of the landowners who at best hired workers. If the "improvement of labor" is the main claim to property rights, then one might fairly suggest that the ones actually doing the labor might have a better claim than those hiring them to perform it. But Section 28 of the *Second Treatise* suggests that Locke did not conceive of "labor" in quite this way, and that the labor of those one has hired can in fact be counted as one's own labor:

> ... the taking of this or that part [of the commons] does not depend on the express consent of all the commoners. Thus the grass my horse has bit; the turf my servant has cut; and the ore I have dug in any place, where I have a right to them in common with others, become my property.

Locke is in this section of his argument talking about material removed from the land (grass, turf, ore) becoming one's property, not the land itself. But if the labor of one's servant in cutting the turf may count as one's own labor in determining ownership of that piece cut from the land, why might it not count as such in determining ownership of the land itself? In Section 37 (added by Locke in later editions of the work), he is more explicit when he asserts of "he that encloses land" that "his labor now supplies him with provisions out of ten acres, which were but the product of an hundred lying in common." Yet those who enclosed the fields rarely performed physical labor on them. Thus many scholars (beginning with C.B. Macpherson in the 1960s[1]) have suggested that, despite sometimes seeming to place significant restrictions on the accumulation of property, Locke is in effect advocating an unrestricted right to accumulate property by those who have the means to do so. It is important to note, however, that he also advocates a restriction on the right to property on the grounds of charity. This is set out in Section 42 of the *First Treatise*: Locke states that "every man [has] a title to so much out of another's plenty, as will keep him from extreme want."

The other primary opposition Locke sets up in arguing for property rights is between highly productive, farmed land and "waste" land. But, in England at least, real world conflicts over enclosures did not involve claims to land that had been unused—that had been, in human terms, going to waste. They had to do with how land already recognized as having value would be used. Interestingly, Locke for the most part steers clear of offering English cases in point as he makes his arguments about property. An exception is the passage in Section 37 quoted from above, in which Locke suggests that the value labor has added to ten acres of cultivated fertile land in Devonshire allow it to be as productive as would "an hundred acres lying in common" in England, or as would a thousand acres "in the wild woods and thee uncultivated waste of America." It was likely not chance that led Locke to choose Devonshire as an example; it had been an area that was among the earliest affected by the enclosure movement—so much so that by 1600 almost all the fertile land in the county had been enclosed. By Locke's time, enclosure in Devon was, in other words, a long-settled issue rather than a source of live controversy. Moreover, it was one geographical area in which greater agricultural productivity seemed to have been successfully achieved; in the late 1500s Richard Hooker (an influential ecclesiastical historian who also left descriptions of Devon and of Cornwall, the neighboring region in far southwest England) described the countryside as he remembered it in his youth—"all forests and full of woods ... and thickets"—in contrast to the land now, with "not many wastes" that had not been "converted and changed into tillage or keeping of sheep."

---

1   Macpherson suggests that the introduction of money is a key element in Locke's argument here. As he reads Locke, the implication is that, when there is "no land left, those without any ... have to sell their labor, for wages, to those who [do have] land"; once that has been done, their labor becomes the landowner's property.

Colonialism

It is not likely by chance that Locke repeatedly uses the areas inhabited by the indigenous people of America as an example of a "waste" land. For Locke, issues of property were as much a real practical concern in America as they were in England. As secretary to the lord proprietors of Carolina (1668-71), Secretary to the Council of Trade and Plantations (1673-74), and member of the Board of Trade (1696) Locke held key positions in bodies that oversaw the progress of the colonization by the British of large areas of the new world. He was employed, in short, to further the interests of the colonizers.

In this connection, Sections 34 and 45 are central to the arguments made in the *Second Treatise*. In the first of these sections Locke qualifies the assertion that "God gave the world to men in common" with the proviso that "he gave it to the use of the industrious and rational." In the second, he contrasts those societies which, "with the use of money" and also by laws and "by compact and agreement," have settled property arrangements among themselves, and those societies which have not done so. The point that Locke emphasizes, interestingly, is not the laws or the compacts and agreements. Rather it is the use of money:

> Yet there are still great tracts of ground to be found, which (the inhabitants thereof not having joined with the rest of mankind, in the consent of the use of their common money) lie waste, and are more than the people who dwell on it ... can make use of, and so still lie in common: though this can scarce happen among that part of mankind that have consented to the use of money.

Locke clearly implies that the right of English colonizers in America to appropriate land to themselves should be unrestricted so long as the "wild Indians" remained a society in which arrangements were not made using the currency of England.

Slavery

Many commentators have suggested that Chapter 4 of the *Second Treatise* stands out as a peculiarity; here the great champion of liberty appears to attempt to justify slavery. Commentators have often noted the seeming incongruity of this with Locke's general views about God-given natural rights and equality for all humans. Though it may be impossible to advance any reading of the arguments in Chapter 4 with complete certainty, it is again helpful to be aware of some historical and biographical background. The English slave trade had begun in the 1550s under the direction of the sea captain Sir John Hawkins. By the late seventeenth century a triangular trade was starting to become well established; English ships would transport captured Africans to become slaves in the Americas (most frequently on sugar or tobacco plantations), and would then carry the products of the plantations from the Americas for sale in Britain. Though some Britons of the time—George Warren is one notable example—lamented that slaves were "sold like dogs, and no better esteemed but for their work-sake, which they perform all their week, with the severest [punishments] for the slightest fault,"[1] popular opinion in the seventeenth century had certainly not for the most part turned against slavery. (Even Aphra Behn's *Orinooko, Or The Royal Slave* (1688), a fictionalized account of a slave rebellion in Surinam that was unusual for its sympathetic portrayal of a black African hero and heroine, did not directly take issue with slavery.)

In recent times several scholars have drawn attention to the role Locke himself played in the development of this trade. He and Shaftesbury were both among those who invested in the Company of Royal Adventurers of England Trading with Africa (commonly referred to as the Royal African Company), which in 1660 had been granted a charter to engage in the slave trade; Locke purchased shares in 1671, and sold them at a profit four years later. Locke was also the chief author of the 1669 *Fundamental Constitutions of Carolina*—a document which included the provision that "every freeman shall have absolute power and authority over his negro slaves of what opinion or religion soever." Moreover (as the historian David Armitage has shown[2]), Locke was involved in a less formal capacity in later revisions of the *Fundamental Constitutions* that retained the provision—including a 1682 revision that was conducted at about the same time Locke is likely to have been completing the *Second Treatise*. And in the *First Treatise* Locke writes with apparent equanimity of a master having power over "slaves bought with money." How can any of this be squared with Locke's arguments concerning "the natural liberty of man"?

Again, an important part of Locke's argument is that certain people deserve more rights than others. In particular, societies in which com-

---

1   *Impartial Description of Surinam* (1667). Surinam was a slave colony on the northern coast of South America, and is now a sovereign state.

2   "John Locke, Carolinas, and the *Two Treatises of Government*." *Political Theory* (32:5, October 2004, 602-27).

pacts and agreements and "consent to the use of money" prevail have special standing. But while Locke seems clearly to have taken that special standing as being associated with a right to appropriate land, he does not appear to have taken it to justify slavery; in 1671 (as Armitage has pointed out), he drafted a provision against the enslavement of Indians in Carolina.

It is notable that Locke's chapter "Of Slavery" makes no specific references to the actual forms of slavery that were being widely practiced in his own time. Are the contortions of Section 23 meant to justify racially-based chattel slavery (of the sort Locke had himself profited from in the West Indies), on the grounds that any such slave is to some extent free so long as he can either kill himself directly or, "by resisting the will of his master, ... draw on himself the death he desires"? Or do slaves from Africa count for Locke (as they did for many at the time) purely as property, without standing as human beings at all? In that case, does Locke mean to discuss only the sort of slavery that has often in human history been imposed by those victorious in war on the vanquished?[1] Or might Locke have had in mind as one reference point the enslavement of close to 100,000 Irish beginning in the 1660s, who were transported by the English as slaves or indentured servants, many of them consigned to work on the sugar plantations of the West Indies? In the end it is easy to find fodder for discussion in Locke's account of slavery, but difficult to settle on clear answers.

Some Common Misconceptions

1. Locke was not an advocate of modern democracy. His view (qualified in several respects) is that government is legitimate when it has the consent of the governed; but this can occur in a variety of political forms. On this view, a monarchy can be legitimate when the monarch has the consent of, and expresses the will of, his or her subjects.
2. Locke is commonly said to be the father of liberalism, but that can be misleading; the word 'liberalism' has undergone several changes in meaning over the centuries, and should be used with care. Characteristics associated with liberalism in Locke's time and somewhat

---

1 Many seventeenth- and early eighteenth-century writers took what is to modern minds a surprisingly matter-of-fact attitude to such slavery. An interesting case in point is Daniel Defoe's novel *Robinson Crusoe* (1719). Much as Crusoe looks to escape from slavery, he no more suggests that his own capture and enslavement (by a group of moors) was morally wrong than he questions his own right to enslave others later in the story.

later (and which apply in his case) include an emphasis on intellectual liberty, a valuing of individual autonomy, a concern for the protection of civil liberties and rights, and a generally optimistic view of the innate character of human beings and of the possibility of social progress. When the word "liberal" is used today it often lacks some or all of these connotations, and carries others.

3. Locke is counted as one of the first of the British Empiricists, but there are several aspects of his thought that are notably anti-empirical. The most notable of these in his political writing is his treatment of natural rights, which (like other ethical truths) he believes are discovered through the operations of rationality alone, not given by the senses.

How Important and Influential Is *The Second Treatise*?

Anthony Quinton, the distinguished contemporary philosopher, writes that Locke "must be acknowledged to be the most influential of political thinkers, above even Plato, Aristotle, Hobbes, Rousseau, and Marx.... [His writings] became something like the sacred text of eighteenth-century Whiggism."[1] Locke's idea that government needs the consent of the governed became the officially accepted view in nations such as Britain. It is perhaps ironic (given Locke's own involvement in colonial projects) that his writings can also be counted as an influence on British voluntary de-colonialization after World War II. His argument that it is legitimate to overthrow a government that no longer has the consent of the governed was probably an influence on the French Revolution, through Voltaire, who admired Locke; and it definitely had an enormous effect on the American revolutionists. Thomas Jefferson was a thoroughgoing Lockean, calling Locke one of "the three greatest men that have ever lived, without any exception."[2] Jefferson's *Declaration of Independence* is Lockean in its insistence

---

1 "Political Philosophy," in Anthony Kenny, ed., *The Oxford Illustrated History of Western Philosophy* (Oxford University Press, 2001), 323. The reference here is to the British Whig Party, the opposition to the Tories. In very general terms, the Whigs represented reformist, parliamentarian, and "liberal" tendencies (see above); they evolved into the Liberal Party (while the Tories, standing for tradition, privilege, and monarchy, evolved into the Conservatives).

2 The other two were Bacon and Newton. Jefferson praised the three for "having laid the foundations of those superstructures which have been raised in the Physical & Moral sciences" (Jefferson's February 15, 1789, letter to John Trumbull, ordering copies of portraits of the three men). Of course, Bacon and Newton were the physical scientists; Locke was the moral scientist.

that government must have the consent of the governed; that rebellion is justified when this consent is missing; in its assertion of the equality of all men; and in its attribution of inalienable natural God-given rights. (Interestingly, the *Declaration* substituted "the pursuit of happiness" for "property" in Locke's "life, liberty, and ... property"; it is sometimes supposed that Jefferson did not want to put the right to own slaves on the same level as the other basic rights.) Locke also had a profound influence on the American Constitution—for example, in the tripartite separation of governmental powers. (Locke's division was 'legislative,' 'executive,' and 'federative'; Montesquieu modified this into the form that appeared in the Constitution by substituting "judicial" for the third division.) Locke's political liberalism is also apparent in many other of its basic features, including the separation of church and state.

The Lockean doctrines of the inborn rights, essential freedom, and natural equality of all humans have been an inspiration for liberals (and for various sorts of radicals) in all eras. The utilitarians Jeremy Bentham and John Stuart Mill show clear signs of his influence. The socialist Thomas Hodgskin invoked Locke in 1832 in support of his plea for the rights of the oppressed laboring man. Surprisingly, Karl Marx is sometimes also counted among those influenced by Locke: Marx's theories of property and value, both constituted by the addition of labor to what is provided by nature, are in some ways similar to Locke's. However, it is obvious that the two thinkers disagree strongly about most matters. Some Marxists have taken Locke to be the quintessential apologist for unbridled free enterprise and private property. Some libertarians claim that their notions of freedom are rooted in a Lockean tradition; others argue that the way in which Locke distinguishes between liberty and license, and embraces law as the natural site of liberty, does not square easily with libertarianism. On virtually all areas of the ideological spectrum, then, there are those whose thinking is rooted in ideas from Locke—but there is clearly no sole heir.

Suggestions for Critical Reflection

1. Is Locke's "state of nature" one that has ever historically existed? Does the question of its historical existence have bearing on Locke's reasoning about the origins of government?
2. Locke claims that in a state of nature we are justified in claiming a natural resource if, in so doing, we leave as much and as good of that resource for others (§ 27). Are there any situations in the modern world in which natural resources can be claimed in this manner?

3. Many of Locke's arguments, including his justifications of the natural right to property and of the equality of persons, are grounded in the idea that we are all the creations of an omnipotent being. Would those arguments hold in the absence of belief in God?

4. Is Locke right to describe uncultivated land, such as that of North America prior to European colonization, as a 'waste' (§ 36-38)? Can such land have value independent of the resources it produces for human consumption? If so, what kind of value? Ethical? Aesthetic?

5. Why does Locke write at length on the limits of parental authority towards children? How does that discussion pertain to his analysis of political authority (Chapter 6)?

6. Do you agree with Locke's claim that "the great and chief end, therefore, of men's uniting into commonwealths, and putting themselves under government, *is the preservation of their property*" (§ 124)? (Keep in mind the definition of 'property' that Locke employs in the preceding section.)

7. Locke claims that one tacitly consents to a government's authority if one has property under that government's jurisdiction, since one is always at liberty not to consent by instead joining another commonwealth or beginning a new one in an area that is "free and unpossessed" (§ 121). However, in practice it may be difficult, if not impossible, to immigrate to a different nation or to find unpossessed land. Does this mean that we are in most cases obligated to consent to the authority of the state we are born into?

8. Why does Locke treat taxation as a special form of legislation that can be justified only by the consent of the majority (§ 138-40)?

9. In his discussion of conquest, Locke emphasizes the importance of a natural right to inherit property from one's ancestors (Chapter 16). Is such a right justified by Locke's reasoning regarding the origins of property? Is it inconsistent with that reasoning?

10. Locke's examination of the conditions under which a government may be dissolved focuses on the form of government with which Locke himself was most familiar—a monarchy with executive power operating alongside hereditary nobility and democratic representatives. How might the conditions of government dissolution differ for some other form of government, such as that in your country?

11. Locke's discussion of government dissolution and revolution was written prior to several of the revolutions now most well-known in the Western world, including the French Revolution and the American Revolution. Would those revolutions be justified, in Locke's view?

Suggestions for Further Reading

Though the *Second Treatise* can be fruitfully read on its own, it was originally published alongside the *First Treatise*; reading the latter can help to clarify the political context in which Locke lived and wrote. The two works are published together as *Two Treatises on Government*.

Another of Locke's central political works is *A Letter Concerning Toleration*. It advocates religious toleration in England—that is, toleration for various Christian denominations. Locke's immediate concern in the *Letter* is the use of the power of the state to coerce "nonconformist" Protestants, such as Presbyterians and Quakers, into the Anglican Church, officially established as the Church of England; and with the practice of persecution and denial of full citizenship to non-members of that church. Locke's argument for the separation of church and state ("the Church itself is a thing absolutely separate and distinct from the Commonwealth"), radical and widely unpopular in Locke's day, has become a mainstay of liberal political sensibility, which wants to limit the concerns of the state to public civil matters.

Locke is known not only for his political writings but also for his influential philosophical work in epistemology (the theory of knowledge) and metaphysics. Central to his writing in these areas is *An Essay Concerning Human Understanding*.

For more information on Locke's life, consider Maurice Cranston's *John Locke: A Biography* (Oxford University Press, 1957) or Roger Woolhouse's *Locke: A Biography* (Cambridge University Press, 2007).

Locke is commonly interpreted as an advocate of "social contract theory"—the idea that political institutions are grounded in or legitimated by the agreement of the people who are governed by those institutions. In this respect, he is preceded in the early modern world by Thomas Hobbes in *Leviathan* (1660), and followed by Jean-Jacques Rousseau in *Discourse on the Origin and Foundations of Inequality among Men* (1755) and *On the Social Contract or Principles of Political Right* (1762). Perhaps the most notable of contemporary social contract theorists is John Rawls, author of the hugely influential *A Theory of Justice* (Harvard University Press, 1971; revised edition 1999).

The Second Treatise of Civil Government

The Second Treatise of Civil Government

Preface[1]

Reader, you have here the beginning and end of a discourse concerning government; what fate has otherwise disposed of the papers that should have filled up the middle, and were more than all the rest, it is not worth while to tell you.[2] These, which remain, I hope are sufficient to establish the throne of our great restorer, our present King William;[3] to make good his title, in the consent of the people, which being the only one of all lawful governments, he has more fully and clearly, than any prince[4] in Christendom; and to justify to the world the people of England, whose love of their just and natural rights, with their resolution to preserve them, saved the nation when it was on the very brink of slavery and ruin. If these papers have that evidence, I flatter myself is to be found in them, there will be no great miss of those which are lost, and my reader may be satisfied without them: for I imagine, I shall have neither the time, nor inclination to repeat my pains, and fill up the wanting[5] part of my answer, by tracing Sir Robert again, through all the windings and obscurities, which are to be met

---

1 *Preface* This is the preface to the whole work (consisting of the *First* and *Second Treatises*). Only the Second is included here.

2 *what fate ... tell you* Some pages that were to go into the *Second Treatise* were simply lost. They contained an extended attack on the arguments of Sir Robert Filmer, an advocate of the divine right of kings, and of their absolute power to rule. Locke's *First Treatise* consists largely of an attack on Filmer, and, as you will see, the Second contains a good deal of this also. It is suspected that the lost pages overlapped this attack considerably.

3 *King William* William of Orange, who took over as king from James II in the Revolution of 1688 (the "Bloodless" or "Glorious" Revolution). William's coming to power is often seen as the beginning of modern English parliamentary government, with limited power for the monarchy.

4 *prince* Ruler.

5 *wanting* Lacking.

with in the several branches of his wonderful system. The king, and body of the nation, have since so thoroughly confuted[1] his hypothesis, that I suppose nobody hereafter will have either the confidence to appear against[2] our common safety, and be again an advocate for slavery; or the weakness to be deceived with contradictions dressed up in a popular style, and well-turned periods:[3] for if anyone will be at the pains, himself, in those parts, which are here untouched, to strip Sir Robert's discourses of the flourish of doubtful[4] expressions, and endeavor to reduce his words to direct, positive,[5] intelligible propositions, and then compare them one with another, he will quickly be satisfied, there was never so much glib nonsense put together in well-sounding English. If he think it not worth while to examine his works all through, let him make an experiment in that part, where he treats of usurpation;[6] and let him try, whether he can, with all his skill, make Sir Robert intelligible, and consistent with himself, or common sense. I should not speak so plainly of a gentleman, long since past answering, had not the pulpit, of late years, publicly owned[7] his doctrine, and made it the current divinity[8] of the times. It is necessary those men, who taking on them to be teachers, have so dangerously misled others, should be openly showed of what authority this their Patriarch is, whom they have so blindly followed, that so they may either retract what upon so ill grounds they have vented, and cannot be maintained; or else justify those principles which they preached up for gospel; though they had no better an author than an English courtier: for I should not have writ against Sir Robert, or taken the pains to show his mistakes, inconsistencies, and want of (what he so much boasts of, and pretends wholly to build on) scripture-proofs, were there not men among us, who, by crying up[9] his books, and espousing his doctrine, save me from the reproach of writing against a dead adversary. They have been so zealous in this point, that, if I have done him any wrong,

---

1   *confuted*   Refuted.
2   *appear against*   Argue against.
3   *well-turned periods*   Beautifully constructed sentences.
4   *doubtful*   Ambiguous.
5   *positive*   Here this word means "clear," but see the note above, in the section "Some Useful Background Information" for other meanings encountered in the text below.
6   *usurpation*   Seizing an office, replacing the previous holder, by force.
7   *the pulpit, of late years, publicly owned*   The Church, recently, publicly adopted.
8   *divinity*   Object of adoration.
9   *crying up*   Praising.

I cannot hope they should spare me. I wish, where they have done the truth and the public wrong, they would be as ready to redress it, and allow its just weight to this reflection, viz. that there cannot be done a greater mischief[1] to prince and people, than the propagating wrong notions concerning government; that so at last all times might not have reason to complain of the Drum Ecclesiastic.[2] If anyone, concerned really for truth, undertake the confutation[3] of my Hypothesis, I promise him either to recant[4] my mistake, upon fair conviction; or to answer his difficulties. But he must remember two things.

First, That caviling[5] here and there, at some expression, or little incident of my discourse, is not an answer to my book.

Secondly, That I shall not take railing[6] for arguments, nor think either of these worth my notice, though I shall always look on myself as bound to give satisfaction to anyone, who shall appear to be conscientiously scrupulous in the point, and shall show any just grounds for his scruples.

I have nothing more, but to advertise[7] the reader, that Observations stands for *Observations on Hobbs, Milton, &c.* and that a bare quotation of pages always means pages of his *Patriarcha*,[8] Edition 1680.

[...]

---

1 *mischief* Injury.
2 *Drum Ecclesiastic* Noisy rumblings from the Church.
3 *confutation* Refutation.
4 *recant* Withdraw, renounce.
5 *caviling* Making trivial objections.
6 *railing* Scolding.
7 *advertise* Announce to.
8 *Observations on Hobbs, Milton, &c.; Patriarcha* Two works by Filmer.

Book 2

[The Second Treatise]

Chapter 1. Of Political Power

§ 1. It having been shown in the foregoing discourse,[1]

1. That Adam[2] had not, either by natural right of fatherhood, or by positive donation[3] from God, any such authority over his children, or dominion[4] over the world, as is pretended:[5]

2. That if he had, his heirs, yet, had no right to it:

3. That if his heirs had, there being no law of nature nor positive law of God that determines which is the right heir in all cases that may arise, the right of succession, and consequently of bearing rule, could not have been certainly determined:

4. That if even that had been determined, yet the knowledge of which is the eldest line of Adam's posterity,[6] being so long since utterly lost, that in the races of mankind and families of the world, there remains not to one above another, the least pretence to be the eldest house,[7] and to have the right of inheritance:

All these premises having, as I think, been clearly made out, it is impossible that the rulers now on earth should make any benefit, or derive any the least shadow of authority from that, which is held to be the fountain[8] of all power, Adam's private dominion and paternal jurisdiction; so that he that will not give just occasion to think that all government in the world is the product only of force and violence, and that men live together by no other rules but that of beasts, where the strongest carries it, and so lay a foundation for perpetual disorder and mischief, tumult, sedition and rebellion, (things that the followers of that hypothesis so loudly cry out against) must of necessity find out another rise[9] of government, another original[10] of political power, and another way of designing and

---

1 *the foregoing discourse* The *First Treatise of Government*.
2 *Adam* According to the *Old Testament*, the first human.
3 *positive donation* Explicit grant.
4 *dominion* Ruling authority.
5 *pretended* Claimed (without warrant).
6 *posterity* Descendants.
7 *eldest house* Line of legitimate heirs (through eldest descendants).
8 *fountain* Source.
9 *so that he ... must of necessity find out another rise* This means: So if you don't want to give reason to think that all government is the product of force and violence (etc.), then you must find another account of its origins.
10 *original* Origin, source.

knowing the persons that have it, than what Sir Robert Filmer has taught us.

§ 2. To this purpose, I think it may not be amiss, to set down what I take to be political power; that the power of a magistrate over a subject may be distinguished from that of a father over his children, a master over his servant, a husband over his wife, and a lord over his slave. All which distinct powers happening sometimes together in the same man, if he be considered under these different relations, it may help us to distinguish these powers one from another, and show the difference betwixt[1] a ruler of a commonwealth,[2] a father of a family, and a captain of a galley.

§ 3. Political power, then, I take to be a right of making laws with penalties of death, and consequently all less penalties, for the regulating and preserving of property, and of employing the force of the community, in the execution of such laws, and in the defense of the commonwealth from foreign injury; and all this only for the public good.

Chapter 2. Of the State of Nature

§ 4. To understand political power right, and derive it from its original, we must consider, what state all men are naturally in, and that is, a state of perfect[3] freedom to order their actions, and dispose of[4] their possessions and persons, as they think fit, within the bounds of the law of nature, without asking leave,[5] or depending upon the will of any other man.

A state also of equality, wherein all the power and jurisdiction is reciprocal,[6] no one having more than another; there being nothing more evident, than that creatures of the same species and rank, promiscuously[7] born to all the same advantages of nature, and the use of the same faculties, should also be equal one among another without subordination or subjection, unless the lord and master of them all[8] should, by any manifest declaration of his will, set one above another, and con-

---

1 *betwixt*   Between.
2 *commonwealth*   Any sort of state or community. See the note on this word in the section "Some Useful Background Information" in the Introduction above.
3 *perfect*   Complete.
4 *dispose of*   Deal with, manage.
5 *leave*   Permission.
6 *reciprocal*   Existing on both (all) sides.
7 *promiscuously*   Indiscriminately, at random.
8 *the lord and master of them all*   God.

fer on him, by an evident and clear appointment, an undoubted right to dominion and sovereignty.

§ 5. This equality of men by nature, the judicious Hooker[1] looks upon as so evident in itself, and beyond all question, that he makes it the foundation of that obligation to mutual love among men, on which he builds the duties they owe one another, and from whence he derives the great maxims of justice and charity. His words are,

The like natural inducement has brought men to know that it is no less their duty, to love others than themselves; for seeing those things which are equal, must needs[2] all have one measure;[3] if I cannot but wish to receive good, even as much at every man's hands, as any man can wish unto his own soul, how should I look to have any part of my desire herein satisfied, unless myself be careful to satisfy the like desire, which is undoubtedly in other men, being of one and the same nature? To have any thing offered them repugnant to this desire, must needs in all respects grieve them as much as me, so that if I do harm, I must look to suffer, there being no reason that others should show greater measure of love to me, than they have by me showed unto them: my desire therefore to be loved of my equals in nature as much as possible may be, imposes upon me a natural duty of bearing to them-ward[4] fully the like affection; from which relation of equality between ourselves and them that are as ourselves, what several rules and canons natural reason has drawn, for direction of life, no man is ignorant. *Eccl. Pol. Lib.* 1.

§ 6. But though this be a state of liberty, yet it is not a state of license: though man in that state have an uncontrollable liberty to dispose of his person or possessions, yet he has not liberty to destroy himself, or so much as any creature in his possession, but where[5] some nobler use than its bare preservation calls for it. The state of nature has a law of nature to govern it, which obliges everyone: and reason, which is that law, teaches all mankind, who will but consult it, that being all equal and independent, no one ought to harm another in his life, health, liberty, or possessions: for men being all the workmanship of one omnipotent, and infinitely wise maker; all the servants of one

---

1 *Hooker* Richard Hooker (1554-1600), influential Anglican theologian. The quotation Locke gives is from his *Of the Lawes of Ecclesiastical Politie.*
2 *must needs* Must.
3 *one measure* A single standard.
4 *to them-ward* Toward them.
5 *but where* Except in circumstances in which.

sovereign master, sent into the world by his order, and about his business; they are his property, whose workmanship they are, made to last during his, not one another's pleasure:[1] and being furnished with like faculties, sharing all in one community of nature, there cannot be supposed any such subordination among us, that may authorize us to destroy one another, as if we were made for one another's uses, as the inferior ranks of creatures are for ours. Everyone, as he is bound to preserve himself, and not to quit his station willfully, so by the like reason, when his own preservation comes not in competition, ought he, as much as he can, to preserve the rest of mankind, and may not, unless it be to do justice on an offender, take away, or impair the life, or what tends to the preservation of the life, the liberty, health, limb, or goods of another.

§ 7. And that[2] all men may be restrained from invading others' rights, and from doing hurt to one another, and the law of nature be observed, which wills the peace and preservation of all mankind, the execution of the law of nature is, in that state, put into every man's hands, whereby everyone has a right to punish the transgressors of that law to such a degree, as may hinder its violation: for the law of nature would, as all other laws that concern men in this world be in vain, if there were nobody that in the state of nature had a power to execute that law, and thereby preserve the innocent and restrain offenders. And if anyone in the state of nature may punish another for any evil he has done, everyone may do so: for in that state of perfect equality, where naturally there is no superiority or jurisdiction of one over another, what any may do in prosecution of that law, everyone must needs have a right to do.

§ 8. And thus, in the state of nature, one man comes by a power over another; but yet no absolute or arbitrary[3] power, to use a criminal, when he has got him in his hands, according to the passionate heats, or boundless extravagancy of his own will; but only to retribute[4] to him, so far as calm reason and conscience dictate, what is proportionate to his transgression, which is so much as may serve for reparation[5] and restraint: for these two are the only reasons, why one man may lawfully do harm to another, which is that we call punishment. In transgressing the law of nature, the offender declares himself to live by

---

1 *during his, not one another's pleasure*   As long as he—not somebody else—wants.
2 *that*   So that.
3 *arbitrary*   See note about this word, which occurs frequently, in the above section "Some Useful Background Information," in the introduction to Locke.
4 *retribute*   Return in retaliation.
5 *reparation*   Compensation for harm done to one.

another rule than that of reason and common equity,[1] which is that measure God has set to the actions of men, for their mutual security; and so he becomes dangerous to mankind, the tie, which is to secure them from injury and violence, being slighted and broken by him. Which being a trespass against the whole species, and the peace and safety of it, provided for by the law of nature, every man upon this score, by the right he has to preserve mankind in general, may restrain, or where it is necessary, destroy things noxious to them, and so may bring such evil on anyone, who has transgressed that law, as may make him repent the doing of it, and thereby deter him, and by his example others, from doing the like mischief. And in the case, and upon this ground, *every man has a right to punish the offender and be executioner of the law of nature.*

§ 9. I doubt not but this will seem a very strange doctrine to some men: but before they condemn it, I desire them to resolve[2] me, by what right any prince or state can put to death, or punish an alien, for any crime he commits in their country. It is certain their laws, by virtue of any sanction they receive from the promulgated[3] will of the legislative, reach not a stranger: they speak not to him, nor, if they did, is he bound to hearken to them. The legislative authority, by which they are in force over the subjects of that commonwealth, has no power over him. Those who have the supreme power of making laws in England, France or Holland, are to an Indian, but like the rest of the world, men without authority: and therefore, if by the law of nature every man has not a power to punish offences against it, as he soberly judges the case to require, I see not how the magistrates of any community can punish an alien of another country; since, in reference to him, they can have no more power than what every man naturally may have over another.

§ 10. Besides the crime which consists in violating the law, and varying from the right rule of reason, whereby a man so far becomes degenerate, and declares himself to quit the principles of human nature, and to be a noxious creature, there is commonly injury done to some person or other, and some other man receives damage by his transgression: in which case he who has received any damage, has, besides the right of punishment common to him with other men, a particular right to seek reparation from him that has done it: and any other person, who finds it just, may also join with him that is injured, and as-

---

1 *common equity* Fairness.
2 *resolve* Solve (a problem) for.
3 *promulgated* Officially declared.

sist him in recovering from the offender so much as may make satisfaction for the harm he has suffered.

§ 11. From these two distinct rights, the one of punishing the crime for restraint, and preventing the like offence, which right of punishing is in every body; the other of taking reparation, which belongs only to the injured party, comes it to pass that the magistrate, who by being magistrate has the common right of punishing put into his hands, can often, where the public good demands not the execution of the law, remit[1] the punishment of criminal offences by his own authority, but yet cannot remit the satisfaction due to any private man for the damage he has received. That, he who has suffered the damage has a right to demand in his own name, and he alone can remit: the damnified[2] person has this power of appropriating to himself the goods or service of the offender, by right of self-preservation, as every man has a power to punish the crime, to prevent its being committed again, by the right he has of preserving all mankind, and doing all reasonable things he can in order to that end: and thus it is, that every man, in the state of nature, has a power to kill a murderer, both to deter others from doing the like injury, which no reparation can compensate, by the example of the punishment that attends it from every body, and also to secure men from the attempts of a criminal, who having renounced reason, the common rule and measure God has given to mankind, has, by the unjust violence and slaughter he has committed upon one, declared war against all mankind, and therefore may be destroyed as a lion or a tiger, one of those wild savage beasts, with whom men can have no society nor security: and upon this is grounded that great law of nature, "Whoso sheddeth man's blood, by man shall his blood be shed."[3] And Cain was so fully convinced, that everyone had a right to destroy such a criminal, that after the murder of his brother, he cries out, "Every one that findeth me, shall slay me";[4] so plain was it written in the hearts of all mankind.

§ 12. By the same reason may a man in the state of nature punish the lesser breaches of that law, it will perhaps be demanded, with death? I answer, each transgression may be punished to that degree, and with so much severity, as will suffice to make it an ill bargain to the offender, give him cause to repent, and terrify others from doing the like. Every offence, that can be committed in the state of nature, may in the state of nature be also punished equally, and as far forth as

---

1   *remit*   Give up, forgive, cancel.
2   *damnified*   Injured.
3   Genesis 9:6.
4   Genesis 4:14.

it may, in a commonwealth: for though it would be besides my present purpose, to enter here into the particulars of the law of nature, or its measures of punishment; yet, it is certain there is such a law, and that too, as intelligible and plain to a rational creature, and a studier of that law, as the positive laws of commonwealths; nay, possibly plainer; as much as reason is easier to be understood, than the fancies and intricate contrivances of men, following contrary and hidden interests put into words; for so truly are a great part of the municipal laws of countries, which are only so far right, as they are founded on the law of nature, by which they are to be regulated and interpreted.

§ 13. To this strange doctrine, viz. That in the state of nature everyone has the executive power of the law of nature, I doubt not but it will be objected, that it is unreasonable for men to be judges in their own cases, that self love will make men partial to themselves and their friends: and on the other side, that ill nature, passion and revenge will carry them too far in punishing others; and hence nothing but confusion and disorder will follow, and that therefore God has certainly appointed government to restrain the partiality and violence of men. I easily grant, that civil government is the proper remedy for the inconveniencies[1] of the state of nature, which must certainly be great, where men may be judges in their own case, since it is easy to be imagined, that he who was so unjust as to do his brother an injury, will scarce be so just as to condemn himself for it: but I shall desire those who make this objection, to remember, that absolute monarchs are but men; and if government is to be the remedy of those evils, which necessarily follow from men's being judges in their own cases, and the state of nature is therefore not to be endured, I desire to know what kind of government that is, and how much better it is than the state of nature, where one man, commanding a multitude, has the liberty to be judge in his own case, and may do to all his subjects whatever he pleases without the least question or control of those who execute his pleasure? and in whatsoever he does, whether led by reason, mistake, or passion, must be submitted to? which men in the state of Nature are not bound to do one to another. And if he that judges, judges amiss in his own or any other case, he is answerable for it to the rest of mankind.

§ 14. It is often asked as a mighty objection, "Where are, or ever were there any men in such a state of nature?" To which it may suffice as an answer at present, that since all princes and rulers of independent governments all through the world, are in a state of nature, it is plain the world never was, nor ever will be, without numbers of men

---

1 *inconveniencies* Unsuitable features. This word did not imply, as it does nowadays, trivial unsuitability because of causing discomfort or annoyance, etc.

in that state. I have named all governors of independent communities, whether they are, or are not, in league with others: for it is not every compact that puts an end to the state of nature between men, but only this one of agreeing together mutually to enter into one community, and make one body politic; other promises, and compacts, men may make one with another, and yet still be in the state of nature. The promises and bargains for truck,[1] &c. between the two men in the desert island, mentioned by Garcilasso de la Vega,[2] in his history of Peru; or between a Swiss and an Indian, in the woods of America, are binding to them, though they are perfectly in a state of nature, in reference to one another: for truth and keeping of faith belongs to men, as men, and not as members of society.

§ 15. To those that say, there were never any men in the state of nature, I will not only oppose the authority of the judicious Hooker, *Eccl. Pol. Lib.* I. sect. 10, where he says,

The laws which have been hitherto mentioned, [i.e., the laws of nature] do bind men absolutely, even as they are men, although they have never any settled fellowship, never any solemn agreement amongst themselves what to do, or not to do: but forasmuch as we are not by ourselves sufficient to furnish ourselves with competent store of things, needful for such a life as our nature doth desire, a life fit for the dignity of man; therefore to supply those defects and imperfections which are in us, as living single and solely by ourselves, we are naturally induced to seek communion and fellowship with others: this was the cause of men's uniting themselves at first in politic societies.

But I moreover affirm, that all men are naturally in that state, and remain so, till by their own consents they make themselves members of some politic society; and I doubt not in the sequel of this discourse, to make it very clear.

Chapter 3. Of the State of War

§ 16. The state of war is a state of enmity[3] and destruction: and therefore declaring by word or action, not a passionate and hasty, but a sedate settled design upon another man's life, puts him in a state of war with him against whom he has declared such an intention, and so has

---

1 *truck* Miscellaneous exchanged goods.
2 *Garcilasso de la Vega* Peruvian historian (1539-1616).
3 *enmity* Hostility.

exposed his life to the other's power to be taken away by him, or anyone that joins with him in his defense, and espouses his quarrel; it being reasonable and just, I should have a right to destroy that which threatens me with destruction: for, by the fundamental law of nature, man being to be preserved as much as possible, when all cannot be preserved, the safety of the innocent is to be preferred: and one may destroy a man who makes war upon him, or has discovered an enmity to his being, for the same reason that he may kill a wolf or a lion; because such men are not under the ties of the common law of reason, have no other rule, but that of force and violence, and so may be treated as beasts of prey, those dangerous and noxious creatures, that will be sure to destroy him whenever he falls into their power.

§ 17. And hence it is, that he who attempts to get another man into his absolute power, does thereby put himself into a state of war with him; it being to be understood as a declaration of a design upon his life: for I have reason to conclude, that he who would get me into his power without my consent, would use me as he pleased when he had got me there, and destroy me too when he had a fancy to it; for nobody can desire to have me in his absolute power, unless it be to compel me by force to that which is against the right of my freedom, i.e., make me a slave. To be free from such force is the only security of my preservation; and reason bids me look on him, as an enemy to my preservation, who would take away that freedom which is the fence to[1] it; so that he who makes an attempt to enslave me, thereby puts himself into a state of war with me. He that, in the state of nature, would take away the freedom that belongs to anyone in that state, must necessarily be supposed to have a foundation of all the rest;[2] as he that in the state of society, would take away the freedom belonging to those of that society or commonwealth, must be supposed to design to take away from them every thing else, and so be looked on as in a state of war.

§ 18. This makes it lawful for a man to kill a thief, who has not in the least hurt him, nor declared any design upon his life, any farther than, by the use of force, so to get him in his power, as to take away his money, or what he pleases, from him; because using force, where he has no right, to get me into his power, let his pretence be what it will, I have no reason to suppose, that he, who would take away my liberty, would not, when he had me in his power, take away every thing else. And therefore it is lawful for me to treat him as one who has put himself into a state of war with me, i.e., kill him if I can; for to that haz-

---

1 *fence to* Barrier or defense against.
2 *have a foundation of all the rest* Have a basis for (taking away) everything else.

ard does he justly expose himself, whoever introduces a state of war, and is aggressor in it.

§ 19. And here we have the plain difference between the state of nature and the state of war, which however some men[1] have confounded,[2] are as far distant, as a state of peace, good will, mutual assistance and preservation, and a state of enmity, malice, violence and mutual destruction, are one from another. Men living together according to reason, without a common superior on earth, with authority to judge between them, is properly the state of nature. But force, or a declared design of force, upon the person of another, where there is no common superior on earth to appeal to for relief, is the state of war: and it is the want of such an appeal gives a man the right of war even against an aggressor, though he be in society and a fellow subject. Thus a thief, whom I cannot harm, but by appeal to the law, for having stolen all that I am worth, I may kill, when he sets on me to rob me but of my horse or coat; because the law, which was made for my preservation, where it cannot interpose to secure my life from present force, which, if lost, is capable of no reparation, permits me my own defense, and the right of war, a liberty to kill the aggressor, because the aggressor allows not time to appeal to our common judge, nor the decision of the law, for remedy in a case where the mischief may be irreparable. Want of a common judge with authority, puts all men in a state of nature: force without right, upon a man's person, makes a state of war, both where there is, and is not, a common judge.

§ 20. But when the actual force is over, the state of war ceases between those that are in society, and are equally on both sides subjected to the fair determination of the law; because then there lies open the remedy of appeal for the past injury, and to prevent future harm: but where no such appeal is, as in the state of nature, for want of positive laws, and judges with authority to appeal to, the state of war once begun, continues, with a right to the innocent party to destroy the other whenever he can, until the aggressor offers peace, and desires reconciliation on such terms as may repair any wrongs he has already done, and secure the innocent for the future; nay, where an appeal to the law, and constituted judges, lies open, but the remedy is denied by a manifest perverting of justice, and a barefaced wresting of the laws to protect or indemnify[3] the violence or injuries of some men, or party of men, there it is hard to imagine any thing but a state of war: for wher-

---

1   *some men*   Locke may be referring to Hobbes here. He is eager to emphasize his difference from Hobbes, who wrote that the state of nature *is* a state of war.

2   *confounded*   Confused.

3   *indemnify*   Reimburse afterwards for.

ever violence is used, and injury done, though by hands appointed to administer justice, it is still violence and injury, however colored with the name, pretences, or forms of law, the end whereof being to protect and redress the innocent, by an unbiased application of it, to all who are under it; wherever that is not bona fide[1] done, war is made upon the sufferers, who having no appeal on earth to right them, they are left to the only remedy in such cases, an appeal to heaven.

§ 21. To avoid this state of war (wherein there is no appeal but to heaven, and wherein every the least difference is apt to end, where there is no authority to decide between the contenders) is one great reason of men's putting themselves into society, and quitting the state of nature: for where there is an authority, a power on earth, from which relief can be had by appeal, there the continuance of the state of war is excluded, and the controversy is decided by that power. Had there been any such court, any superior jurisdiction on earth, to determine the right between Jephtha and the Ammonites,[2] they had never come to a state of war: but we see he was forced to appeal to heaven. The Lord the Judge (says he) be judge this day between the children of Israel and the children of Ammon, Judg. xi. 27. and then prosecuting, and relying on his appeal, he leads out his army to battle: and therefore in such controversies, where the question is put, who shall be judge? It cannot be meant, who shall decide the controversy; everyone knows what Jephtha here tells us, that the Lord the Judge shall judge. Where there is no judge on earth, the appeal lies to God in heaven. That question then cannot mean, who shall judge, whether another has put himself in a state of war with me, and whether I may, as Jephtha did, appeal to heaven in it? of that I myself can only be judge in my own conscience, as I will answer it, at the great day, to the supreme judge of all men.

Chapter 4. Of Slavery

§ 22. The natural liberty of man is to be free from any superior power on earth, and not to be under the will or legislative authority of man, but to have only the law of nature for his rule. The liberty of man, in society, is to be under no other legislative power, but that established,

---

1 *bona fide* In good faith.

2 *Jephtha and the Ammonites* In the book of Judges, the Israelites, living under the rule of the Ammonites, get Jephtha to lead them in battle for their freedom. Jephtha agrees, on condition that he will be made king if successful. He appeals to God to judge the justice of the Israelites' cause, wins the battle, and frees the Israelites. This story is important to Locke, who discusses it again in Section 109, below.

by consent, in the commonwealth; nor under the dominion of any will, or restraint of any law, but what that legislative shall enact, according to the trust put in it. Freedom then is not what Sir Robert Filmer tells us, "a liberty for everyone to do what he lists,[1] to live as he pleases, and not to be tied by any laws":[2] but freedom of men under government is, to have a standing rule to live by, common to everyone of that society, and made by the legislative power erected in it; a liberty to follow my own will in all things, where the rule prescribes not; and not to be subject to the inconstant, uncertain, unknown, arbitrary will of another man: as freedom of nature is, to be under no other restraint but the law of nature.

§ 23. This freedom from absolute, arbitrary power, is so necessary to, and closely joined with a man's preservation, that he cannot part with it, but by what forfeits his preservation and life together: for a man, not having the power of his own life, cannot, by compact, or his own consent, enslave himself to anyone, nor put himself under the absolute, arbitrary power of another, to take away his life, when he pleases. Nobody can give more power than he has himself; and he that cannot take away his own life, cannot give another power over it. Indeed, having by his fault forfeited his own life, by some act that deserves death; he, to whom he has forfeited it, may (when he has him in his power) delay to take it, and make use of him to his own service, and he does him no injury by it: for, whenever he finds the hardship of his slavery outweigh the value of his life, it is in his power, by resisting the will of his master, to draw on himself the death he desires.

§ 24. This is the perfect condition of slavery, which is nothing else, but the state of war continued, between a lawful conqueror and a captive: for, if once compact enter between them, and make an agreement for a limited power on the one side, and obedience on the other, the state of war and slavery ceases, as long as the compact endures: for, as has been said, no man can, by agreement, pass over to another that which he has not in himself, a power over his own life.

I confess, we find among the Jews, as well as other nations, that men did sell themselves; but, it is plain, this was only to drudgery, not to slavery: for, it is evident, the person sold was not under an absolute, arbitrary, despotical power: for the master could not have power to kill him, at any time, whom, at a certain time, he was obliged to let go free out of his service; and the master of such a servant was so far from having an arbitrary power over his life, that he could not, at pleasure,

---

1   *what he lists*   That which he is inclined to do.
2   *a liberty for ... laws*   From Filmer's *Observations upon Aristotle's Politiques Touching Forms of Government* (1652), p. 55.

so much as maim him, but the loss of an eye, or tooth, set him free, Exodus 21.[1]

Chapter 5. Of Property

§ 25. Whether we consider natural reason, which tells us, that men, being once born, have a right to their preservation, and consequently to meat and drink, and such other things as nature affords for their subsistence: or revelation, which gives us an account of those grants God made of the world to Adam, and to Noah, and his sons, it is very clear, that God, as king David says, Psalm 115.16.[2] "has given the earth to the children of men"; given it to mankind in common. But this being supposed, it seems to some a very great difficulty, how anyone should ever come to have a property in any thing: I will not content myself to answer, that if it be difficult to make out property, upon a supposition that God gave the world to Adam, and his posterity in common, it is impossible that any man, but one universal monarch, should have any property upon a supposition, that God gave the world to Adam, and his heirs in succession, exclusive of all the rest of his posterity. But I shall endeavor to show, how men might come to have a property in[3] several parts of that which God gave to mankind in common, and that without any express compact of all the commoners.[4]

§ 26. God, who has given the world to men in common, has also given them reason to make use of it to the best advantage of life, and convenience.[5] The earth, and all that is therein, is given to men for the support and comfort of their being. And though all the fruits it naturally produces, and beasts it feeds, belong to mankind in common, as they are produced by the spontaneous hand of nature; and nobody has originally a private dominion, exclusive of the rest of mankind, in any of them, as they are thus in their natural state: yet being given for the use of men, there must of necessity be a means to appropriate[6] them some way or other, before they can be of any use, or at all beneficial to any particular man. The fruit, or venison, which nourishes the wild Indian,

---

1 *Exodus 21* "And if a man smite the eye of his servant, or the eye of his maid, that it perish; he shall let him go free for his eye's sake. And if he smite out his manservant's tooth, or his maidservant's tooth; he shall let him go free for his tooth's sake" (Exodus 21.26-27).

2 *Psalm 115.16* "The heaven, even the heavens, are the LORD's: but the earth has he given to the children of men" (Psalm 115, line 16).

3 *have a property in* Own.

4 *commoners* Those who own the land in common.

5 *convenience* Suitability.

6 *appropriate* Come to own.

who knows no enclosure, and is still a tenant in common, must be his, and so his, i.e., a part of him, that another can no longer have any right to it, before it can do him any good for the support of his life.

§ 27. Though the earth, and all inferior creatures, be common to all men, yet every man has a property in his own person: this nobody has any right to but himself. The labor of his body, and the work of his hands, we may say, are properly his. Whatsoever then he removes out of the state that nature has provided, and left it in, he has mixed his labor with, and joined to it something that is his own, and thereby makes it his property. It being by him removed from the common state nature has placed it in, it has by this labor something annexed to it, that excludes the common right of other men: for this labor being the unquestionable property of the laborer, no man but he can have a right to what that is once joined to, at least where there is enough, and as good, left in common for others.

§ 28. He that is nourished by the acorns he picked up under an oak, or the apples he gathered from the trees in the wood, has certainly appropriated them to himself. Nobody can deny but the nourishment is his. I ask then, when did they begin to be his? when he digested? or when he eat? or when he boiled? or when he brought them home? or when he picked them up? and it is plain, if the first gathering made them not his, nothing else could. That labor put a distinction between them and common: that added something to them more than nature, the common mother of all, had done; and so they became his private right. And will anyone say, he had no right to those acorns or apples, he thus appropriated, because he had not the consent of all mankind to make them his? Was it a robbery thus to assume to himself what belonged to all in common? If such a consent as that was necessary, man had starved, notwithstanding the plenty God had given him. We see in commons, which remain so by compact,[1] that it is the taking any part of what is common, and removing it out of the state nature leaves it in, which begins the property; without which the common is of no use. And the taking of this or that part, does not depend on the express consent of all the commoners. Thus the grass my horse has bit; the turfs[2] my servant has cut; and the ore I have dug in any place, where I have a right to them in common with others, become my property, without the assignation or consent of anybody. The labor that was mine, removing them out of that common state they were in, has fixed my property in them.

---

1   *by compact*   By (legal) agreement.
2   *turfs*   Peat, used for fuel.

§ 29. By making an explicit consent of every commoner, necessary to anyone's appropriating to himself any part of what is given in common, children or servants could not cut the meat, which their father or master had provided for them in common, without assigning to everyone his peculiar part. Though the water running in the fountain be everyone's, yet who can doubt, but that in the pitcher is his only who drew it out? His labor has taken it out of the hands of nature, where it was common, and belonged equally to all her children, and has thereby appropriated it to himself.

§ 30. Thus this law of reason makes the deer that Indian's who has killed it; it is allowed to be his goods, who has bestowed his labor upon it, though before it was the common right of everyone. And among those who are counted the civilized part of mankind, who have made and multiplied positive laws to determine property, this original law of nature, for the beginning of property, in what was before common, still takes place; and by virtue thereof, what fish anyone catches in the ocean, that great and still remaining common of mankind; or what ambergris[1] anyone takes up here, is by the labor that removes it out of that common state nature left it in, made his property, who takes that pains about it. And even among us, the hare that anyone is hunting, is thought his who pursues her during the chase: for being a beast that is still looked upon as common, and no man's private possession; whoever has employed so much labor about any of that kind, as to find and pursue her, has thereby removed her from the state of nature, wherein she was common, and has begun a property.

§ 31. It will perhaps be objected to this, that "if gathering the acorns, or other fruits of the earth, &c. makes a right to them, then anyone may ingross[2] as much as he will." To which I answer, Not so. The same law of nature, that does by this means give us property, does also bound that property too. "God has given us all things richly" 1 Tim. 6.12.[3] is the voice of reason confirmed by inspiration. But how far has he given it us? To enjoy. As much as anyone can make use of to any advantage of life before it spoils, so much he may by his labor fix a property in: whatever is beyond this, is more than his share, and belongs to others. Nothing was made by God for man to spoil or destroy. And thus, considering the plenty of natural provisions there was

---

1 *ambergris*   A waxy substance, secreted by sperm whales, used in making perfume. It is found on beaches or floating on the ocean.

2 *ingross*   Collect in large scale.

3 *1 Tim. 6.12*   "Charge them that are rich in this world, that they be not highminded, nor trust in uncertain riches, but in the living God, who giveth us richly all things to enjoy." 1 Timothy 6:17. 'Highminded' here means haughty, proud, arrogant.

a long time in the world, and the few spenders; and to how small a part of that provision the industry of one man could extend itself, and ingross it to the prejudice[1] of others; especially keeping within the bounds, set by reason, of what might serve for his use; there could be then little room for quarrels or contentions about property so established.

§ 32. But the chief matter of property being now not the fruits of the earth, and the beasts that subsist on it, but the earth itself; as that which takes in and carries with it all the rest; I think it is plain, that property in that too is acquired as the former. As much land as a man tills, plants, improves, cultivates, and can use the product of, so much is his property. He by his labor does, as it were, enclose it from the common. Nor will it invalidate his right, to say every body else has an equal title to it; and therefore he cannot appropriate, he cannot enclose, without the consent of all his fellow-commoners, all mankind. God, when he gave the world in common to all mankind, commanded man also to labor, and the penury of his condition required it of him. God and his reason commanded him to subdue the earth, i.e., improve it for the benefit of life, and therein lay out something upon it that was his own, his labor. He that in obedience to this command of God, subdued, tilled and sowed any part of it, thereby annexed to it something that was his property, which another had no title to, nor could without injury take from him.

§ 33. Nor was this appropriation of any parcel of land, by improving it, any prejudice to any other man, since there was still enough, and as good left; and more than the yet unprovided could use. So that, in effect, there was never the less left for others because of his enclosure for himself: for he that leaves as much as another can make use of, does as good as take nothing at all. Nobody could think himself injured by the drinking of another man, though he took a good draught, who had a whole river of the same water left him to quench his thirst: and the case of land and water, where there is enough of both, is perfectly the same.

§ 34. God gave the world to men in common; but since he gave it them for their benefit, and the greatest conveniences of life they were capable to draw from it, it cannot be supposed he meant it should always remain common and uncultivated. He gave it to the use of the industrious and rational, (and labor was to be his title to it;) not to the fancy or covetousness of the quarrelsome and contentious. He that had as good left for his improvement, as was already taken up, needed not complain, ought not to meddle with what was already improved by

---

1 *prejudice*   Disadvantage or harm.

another's labor: if he did, it is plain he desired the benefit of another's pains, which he had no right to, and not the ground which God had given him in common with others to labor on, and whereof there was as good left, as that already possessed, and more than he knew what to do with, or his industry could reach to.

§ 35. It is true, in land that is common in England, or any other country, where there is plenty of people under government, who have money and commerce, no one can enclose or appropriate any part, without the consent of all his fellow-commoners; because this is left common by compact, i.e., by the law of the land, which is not to be violated. And though it be common, in respect of some men, it is not so to all mankind; but is the joint property of this country, or this parish. Besides, the remainder, after such enclosure, would not be as good to the rest of the commoners, as the whole was when they could all make use of the whole; whereas in the beginning and first peopling of the great common of the world, it was quite otherwise. The law man was under, was rather for appropriating. God commanded, and his wants forced him to labor. That was his property which could not be taken from him wherever he had fixed it. And hence subduing or cultivating the earth, and having dominion, we see are joined together. The one gave title to the other. So that God, by commanding to subdue, gave authority so far to appropriate: and the condition of human life, which requires labor and materials to work on, necessarily introduces private possessions.

§ 36. The measure of property nature has well set by the extent of men's labor and the conveniences of life: no man's labor could subdue, or appropriate all; nor could his enjoyment consume more than a small part; so that it was impossible for any man, this way, to entrench[1] upon the right of another, or acquire to himself a property, to the prejudice of his neighbor, who would still have room for as good, and as large a possession (after the other had taken out his) as before it was appropriated. This measure did confine every man's possession to a very moderate proportion, and such as he might appropriate to himself, without injury to anybody, in the first ages of the world, when men were more in danger to be lost, by wandering from their company, in the then vast wilderness of the earth, than to be straitened[2] for want of room to plant in. And the same measure may be allowed still without prejudice to anybody, as full as the world seems: for supposing a man, or family, in the state they were at first peopling of the world by the children of Adam, or Noah; let him plant in some inland, vacant places

---

1 *entrench* Trespass.
2 *straitened* Restricted.

of America, we shall find that the possessions he could make himself, upon the measures we have given, would not be very large, nor, even to this day, prejudice the rest of mankind, or give them reason to complain, or think themselves injured by this man's encroachment, though the race of men have now spread themselves to all the corners of the world, and do infinitely exceed the small number [it] was at the beginning. Nay, the extent of ground is of so little value, without labor, that I have heard it affirmed, that in Spain itself a man may be permitted to plough, sow and reap, without being disturbed, upon land he has no other title to, but only his making use of it. But, on the contrary, the inhabitants think themselves beholden to him, who, by his industry on neglected, and consequently waste land, has increased the stock of corn,[1] which they wanted. But be this as it will, which I lay no stress on; this I dare boldly affirm, that the same rule of propriety, (viz.) that every man should have as much as he could make use of, would hold still in the world, without straitening anybody; since there is land enough in the world to suffice double the inhabitants, had not the invention of money, and the tacit[2] agreement of men to put a value on it, introduced (by consent) larger possessions, and a right to them; which, how it has done, I shall by and by show more at large.

§ 37. This is certain, that in the beginning, before the desire of having more than man needed had altered the intrinsic value of things, which depends only on their usefulness to the life of man; or had agreed, that a little piece of yellow metal, which would keep without wasting or decay, should be worth a great piece of flesh,[3] or a whole heap of corn; though men had a right to appropriate, by their labor, each one of himself, as much of the things of nature, as he could use: yet this could not be much, nor to the prejudice of others, where the same plenty was still left to those who would use the same industry. To which let me add, that he who appropriates land to himself by his labor, does not lessen, but increase the common stock of mankind: for the provisions serving to the support of human life, produced by one acre of enclosed and cultivated land, are (to speak much within compass[4]) ten times more than those which are yielded by an acre of land of an equal richness lying waste in common. And therefore he that encloses land, and has a greater plenty of the conveniences of life from ten acres, than he could have from an hundred left to nature, may truly be

---

1   *corn*   In Locke's time, "corn" could refer to any type of grain.
2   *tacit*   By understanding or implication, as opposed to open statement.
3   *flesh*   Meat.
4   *much within compass*   Quite within the bounds of moderation—that is, estimating very conservatively.

said to give ninety acres to mankind: for his labor now supplies him with provisions out of ten acres, which were but the product of an hundred lying in common. I have here rated the improved land very low, in making its product but as ten to one, when it is much nearer an hundred to one: for I ask, whether in the wild woods and uncultivated waste of America, left to nature, without any improvement, tillage or husbandry, a thousand acres yield the needy and wretched inhabitants as many conveniences of life, as ten acres of equally fertile land do in Devonshire, where they are well cultivated?

Before the appropriation of land, he who gathered as much of the wild fruit, killed, caught, or tamed, as many of the beasts, as he could; he that so employed his pains about any of the spontaneous products of nature, as any way to alter them from the state which nature put them in, by placing any of his labor on them, did thereby acquire a propriety in them: but if they perished, in his possession, without their due use; if the fruits rotted, or the venison putrefied, before he could spend[1] it, he offended against the common law of nature, and was liable to be punished; he invaded his neighbor's share, for he had no right, farther than his use called for any of them, and they might serve to afford him conveniences of life.

§ 38. The same measures governed the possession of land too: whatsoever he tilled and reaped, laid up and made use of, before it spoiled, that was his peculiar right; whatsoever he enclosed, and could feed, and make use of, the cattle and product was also his. But if either the grass of his enclosure rotted on the ground, or the fruit of his planting perished without gathering, and laying up, this part of the earth, notwithstanding his enclosure, was still to be looked on as waste, and might be the possession of any other. Thus, at the beginning, Cain might take as much ground as he could till, and make it his own land, and yet leave enough to Abel's sheep to feed on; a few acres would serve for both their possessions. But as families increased, and industry enlarged their stocks, their possessions enlarged with the need of them; but yet it was commonly without any fixed property in the ground they made use of, till they incorporated, settled themselves together, and built cities; and then, by consent, they came in time, to set out the bounds of their distinct territories, and agree on limits between them and their neighbors; and by laws within themselves, settled the properties of those of the same society: for we see, that in that part of the world which was first inhabited, and therefore like to be best peopled, even as low down as[2] Abraham's time, they wandered with their

---

1 *spend* Consume.
2 *as low down as* As late as.

flocks, and their herds, which was their substance, freely up and down; and this Abraham did, in a country where he was a stranger. Whence it is plain, that at least a great part of the land lay in common; that the inhabitants valued it not, nor claimed property in any more than they made use of. But when there was not room enough in the same place, for their herds to feed together, they by consent, as Abraham and Lot did, Gen. xiii. 5. separated and enlarged their pasture, where it best liked them. And for the same reason Esau went from his father, and his brother, and planted in mount Seir, Gen. xxxvi. 6.

§ 39. And thus, without supposing any private dominion, and property in Adam, over all the world, exclusive of all other men, which can no way be proved, nor anyone's property be made out from it; but supposing the world given, as it was, to the children of men in common, we see how labor could make men distinct titles to several parcels of it, for their private uses; wherein there could be no doubt of right, no room for quarrel.

§ 40. Nor is it so strange, as perhaps before consideration it may appear, that the property of labor should be able to over-balance the community of land: for it is labor indeed that puts the difference of value on every thing; and let anyone consider what the difference is between an acre of land planted with tobacco or sugar, sown with wheat or barley, and an acre of the same land lying in common, without any husbandry upon it,[1] and he will find, that the improvement of labor makes the far greater part of the value. I think it will be but a very modest computation to say, that of the products of the earth useful to the life of man nine tenths are the effects of labor: nay, if we will rightly estimate things as they come to our use, and cast up the several expenses about them, what in them is purely owing to nature, and what to labor, we shall find, that in most of them ninety-nine hundredths are wholly to be put on the account of labor.

§ 41. There cannot be a clearer demonstration of any thing, than several nations of the Americans are of this; who are rich in land, and poor in all the comforts of life; whom nature having furnished as liberally as any other people, with the materials of plenty, i.e., a fruitful soil, apt to produce in abundance, what might serve for food, raiment,[2] and delight; yet for want of improving it by labor, have not one hundredth part of the conveniences we enjoy: and a king of a large and fruitful territory there, feeds, lodges, and is clad worse than a day-laborer in England.

---

1   *without any husbandry upon it*   Unfarmed.
2   *raiment*   Clothing.

§ 42. To make this a little clearer, let us but trace some of the ordinary provisions of life, through their several progresses, before they come to our use, and see how much they receive of their value from human industry. Bread, wine and cloth, are things of daily use, and great plenty; yet notwithstanding, acorns, water and leaves, or skins, must be our bread, drink and clothing, did not labor furnish us with these more useful commodities: for whatever bread is more worth than acorns, wine than water, and cloth or silk, than leaves, skins or moss, that is wholly owing to labor and industry; the one of these being the food and raiment which unassisted nature furnishes us with; the other, provisions which our industry and pains prepare for us, which how much they exceed the other in value, when anyone has computed, he will then see how much labor makes the far greatest part of the value of things we enjoy in this world: and the ground which produces the materials, is scarce to be reckoned in, as any, or at most, but a very small part of it; so little, that even among us, land that is left wholly to nature, that has no improvement of pasturage, tillage, or planting, is called, as indeed it is, waste; and we shall find the benefit of it amount to little more than nothing.

This shows how much numbers of men are to be preferred to largeness of dominions; and that the increase of lands, and the right employing of them, is the great art of government: and that prince, who shall be so wise and godlike, as by established laws of liberty to secure protection and encouragement to the honest industry of mankind, against the oppression of power and narrowness of party, will quickly be too hard for his neighbors: but this by the by.[1] To return to the argument in hand,

§ 43. An acre of land, that bears here twenty bushels of wheat, and another in America, which, with the same husbandry, would do the like, are, without doubt, of the same natural intrinsic value: but yet the benefit mankind receives from the one in a year, is worth five pounds and from the other possibly not worth a penny, if all the profit an Indian received from it were to be valued, and sold here; at least, I may truly say, not one thousandth. It is labor then which puts the greatest part of value upon land, without which it would scarcely be worth any thing: it is to that we owe the greatest part of all its useful products; for all that the straw, bran, bread, of that acre of wheat, is more worth than the product of an acre of as good land, which lies waste, is all the effect of labor: for it is not barely[2] the plough-man's pains, the reaper's and thresher's toil, and the baker's sweat, [that] is to be counted into

---

1 *by the by* After a while. Locke means that he will return to this subject later.
2 *barely* merely.

the bread we eat; the labor of those who broke the oxen, who dug and wrought the iron and stones, who felled and framed the timber employed about the plough, mill, oven, or any other utensils, which are a vast number, requisite to this corn, from its being feed to be sown to its being made bread, must all be charged on the account of labor, and received as an effect of that: nature and the earth furnished only the almost worthless materials, as in themselves. It would be a strange catalogue of things, that industry provided and made use of, about every loaf of bread, before it came to our use, if we could trace them; iron, wood, leather, bark, timber, stone, bricks, coals, lime, cloth, dyeing drugs,[1] pitch, tar, masts, ropes, and all the materials made use of in the ship, that brought any of the commodities made use of by any of the workmen, to any part of the work; all which it would be almost impossible, at least too long, to reckon up.

§ 44. From all which it is evident, that though the things of nature are given in common, yet man, by being master of himself, and proprietor of his own person, and the actions or labor of it, had still in himself the great foundation of property; and that, which made up the great part of what he applied to the support or comfort of his being, when invention and arts had improved the conveniences of life, was perfectly his own, and did not belong in common to others.

§ 45. Thus labor, in the beginning, gave a right of property, wherever anyone was pleased to employ it upon what was common, which remained a long while the far greater part, and is yet more than mankind makes use of. Men, at first, for the most part, contented themselves with what unassisted nature offered to their necessities: and though afterwards, in some parts of the world, (where the increase of people and stock, with the use of money, had made land scarce, and so of some value) the several communities settled the bounds of their distinct territories, and by laws within themselves regulated the properties of the private men of their society, and so, by compact and agreement, settled the property which labor and industry began; and the leagues that have been made between several states and kingdoms, either expressly or tacitly disowning all claim and right to the land in the others' possession, have, by common consent, given up their pretenses to their natural common right, which originally they had to those countries, and so have, by positive agreement, settled a property among themselves, in distinct parts and parcels of the earth; yet there are still great tracts of ground to be found, which (the inhabitants thereof not having joined with the rest of mankind, in the consent of the use of their common money) lie waste, and are more than the peo-

---

1   *dyeing drugs*   Chemicals for dyeing (coloring cloth).

ple who dwell on it do, or can make use of, and so still lie in common; though this can scarce happen among that part of mankind that have consented to the use of money.

§ 46. The greatest part[1] of things really useful to the life of man, and such as the necessity of subsisting made the first commoners of the world look after, as it does the Americans now, are generally things of short duration; such as, if they are not consumed by use, will decay and perish of themselves: gold, silver and diamonds, are things that fancy[2] or agreement has put the value on, more than real use, and the necessary support of life. Now of those good things which nature has provided in common, everyone had a right (as has been said) to as much as he could use, and property in all that he could effect with his labor; all that his industry could extend to, to alter from the state nature had put it in, was his. He that gathered a hundred bushels of acorns or apples, had thereby a property in them, they were his goods as soon as gathered. He was only to look, that he used them before they spoiled, else he took more than his share, and robbed others. And indeed it was a foolish thing, as well as dishonest, to hoard up more than he could make use of. If he gave away a part to anybody else, so that it perished not uselessly in his possession, these he also made use of. And if he also bartered away plums, that would have rotted in a week, for nuts that would last good for his eating a whole year, he did no injury; he wasted not the common stock; destroyed no part of the portion of goods that belonged to others, so long as nothing perished uselessly in his hands. Again, if he would give his nuts for a piece of metal, pleased with its color; or exchange his sheep for shells, or wool for a sparkling pebble or a diamond, and keep those by him all his life he invaded not the right of others, he might heap up as much of these durable things as he pleased; the exceeding of the bounds of his just property not lying in the largeness of his possession, but the perishing of any thing uselessly in it.

§ 47. And thus came in the use of money, some lasting thing that men might keep without spoiling, and that by mutual consent men would take in exchange for the truly useful, but perishable supports of life.

§ 48. And as different degrees of industry were apt to give men possessions in different proportions, so this invention of money gave them the opportunity to continue and enlarge them:[3] for supposing an island, separate from all possible commerce with the rest of the world,

---

1 *greatest part*   Majority.
2 *fancy*   Liking or desire.
3 *enlarge them*   Acquire more possessions.

wherein there were but an hundred families, but there were sheep, horses and cows, with other useful animals, wholesome fruits, and land enough for corn for a hundred thousand times as many, but nothing in the island, either because of its commonness, or perishableness, fit to supply the place of money; what reason could anyone have there to enlarge his possessions beyond the use of his family, and a plentiful supply to its consumption, either in what their own industry produced, or they could barter for like perishable, useful commodities, with others? Where there is not some thing, both lasting and scarce, and so valuable to be hoarded up, there men will not be apt to enlarge their possessions of land, were it never so rich, never so free for them to take: for I ask, what would a man value ten thousand, or an hundred thousand acres of excellent land, ready cultivated, and well stocked too with cattle, in the middle of the inland parts of America, where he had no hopes of commerce with other parts of the world, to draw money to him by the sale of the product? It would not be worth the enclosing, and we should see him give up again to the wild common of nature, whatever was more than would supply the conveniences of life to be had there for him and his family.

§ 49. Thus in the beginning all the world was America, and more so than that is now; for no such thing as money was anywhere known. Find out something that has the use and value of money among his neighbors, you shall see the same man will begin presently[1] to enlarge his possessions.

§ 50. But since gold and silver, being little useful to the life of man in proportion to food, raiment, and carriage,[2] has its value only from the consent of men, whereof labor yet makes, in great part, the measure, it is plain, that men have agreed to a disproportionate and unequal possession of the earth, they having, by a tacit and voluntary consent, found out, a way how a man may fairly possess more land than he himself can use the product of, by receiving in exchange for the overplus[3] gold and silver, which may be hoarded up without injury to anyone; these metals not spoiling or decaying in the hands of the possessor. This partage[4] of things in an inequality of private possessions, men have made practicable[5] out of the bounds of society, and without compact, only by putting a value on gold and silver, and tacitly agreeing in the use of money: for in governments, the laws regu-

---

1 *presently*   Immediately.
2 *carriage*   Transport.
3 *overplus*   Surplus.
4 *partage*   Division.
5 *practicable*   Doable.

late the right of property, and the possession of land is determined by positive constitutions.

§ 51. And thus, I think, it is very easy to conceive, without any difficulty, how labor could at first begin a title of property in the common things of nature, and how the spending it upon our uses bounded it. So that there could then be no reason of quarrelling about title, nor any doubt about the largeness of possession it gave. Right and conveniency went together; for as a man had a right to all he could employ his labor upon, so he had no temptation to labor for more than he could make use of. This left no room for controversy about the title, nor for encroachment on the right of others; what portion a man carved to himself, was easily seen; and it was useless, as well as dishonest, to carve himself too much, or take more than he needed.

Chapter 6. Of Paternal Power

§ 52. It may perhaps be censured as an impertinent[1] criticism, in a discourse of this nature, to find fault with words and names, that have obtained in the world: and yet possibly it may not be amiss to offer new ones, when the old are apt to lead men into mistakes, as this of paternal power probably has done, which seems so to place the power of parents over their children wholly in the father, as if the mother had no share in it; whereas, if we consult reason or revelation, we shall find, she has an equal title. This may give one reason to ask, whether this might not be more properly called parental power? for whatever obligation nature and the right of generation lays on children, it must certainly bind them equal to both the concurrent causes of it. And accordingly we see the positive law of God every where joins them together, without distinction, when it commands the obedience of children, "Honor thy father and thy mother" (Exod. xx. 12); "Whosoever curseth his father or his mother" (Lev. xx. 9); "Ye shall fear every man his mother and his father" (Lev. xix. 3); "Children, obey your parents," &c. (Eph. vi. 1), is the style of the Old and New Testament.

§ 53. Had but this one thing been well considered, without looking any deeper into the matter, it might perhaps have kept men from running into those gross mistakes, they have made, about this power of parents; which, however it might, without any great harshness, bear the name of absolute dominion, and regal authority, when under the title of paternal power it seemed appropriated to the father, would yet have sounded but oddly, and in the very name shown the absurdity, if this supposed absolute power over children had been called parental; and

---

1 *impertinent* Irrelevant.

thereby have discovered, that it belonged to the mother too: for it will but very ill serve the turn of those men, who contend so much for the absolute power and authority of the fatherhood, as they call it, that the mother should have any share in it; and it would have but ill supported the monarchy they contend for, when by the very name it appeared, that that fundamental authority, from whence they would derive their government of a single person only, was not placed in one, but two persons jointly. But to let this of names pass.

§ 54. Though I have said above, (Chapter II) That all men by nature are equal, I cannot be supposed to understand all sorts of equality: age or virtue may give men a just precedency:[1] excellency of parts and merit may place others above the common level: birth may subject some, and alliance or benefits others, to pay an observance to those to whom nature, gratitude, or other respects, may have made it due: and yet all this consists with the equality, which all men are in, in respect of jurisdiction or dominion one over another; which was the equality I there spoke of, as proper to the business in hand, being that equal right, that every man has, to his natural freedom, without being subjected to the will or authority of any other man.

§ 55. Children, I confess, are not born in this full state of equality, though they are born to it. Their parents have a sort of rule and jurisdiction over them, when they come into the world, and for some time after; but it is but a temporary one. The bonds of this subjection are like the swaddling clothes they are wrapped up in, and supported by, in the weakness of their infancy: age and reason as they grow up, loosen them, till at length they drop quite off, and leave a man at his own free disposal.

§ 56. Adam was created a perfect man, his body and mind in full possession of their strength and reason, and so was capable, from the first instant of his being to provide for his own support and preservation, and govern his actions according to the dictates of the law of reason which God had implanted in him. From him the world is peopled with his descendants, who are all born infants, weak and helpless, without knowledge or understanding: but to supply the defects of this imperfect state, till the improvement of growth and age has removed them, Adam and Eve, and after them all parents were, by the law of nature, under an obligation to preserve, nourish, and educate the children they had begotten; not as their own workmanship, but the workmanship of their own Maker, the Almighty, to whom they were to be accountable for them.

---

1   *precedency*   Superiority.

§ 57. The law, that was to govern Adam, was the same that was to govern all his posterity, the law of reason. But his offspring having another way of entrance into the world, different from him, by a natural birth, that produced them ignorant and without the use of reason, they were not presently under that law; for nobody can be under a law, which is not promulgated to him; and this law being promulgated or made known by reason only, he that is not come to the use of his reason, cannot be said to be under this law; and Adam's children, being not presently as soon as born under this law of reason, were not presently free: for law, in its true notion, is not so much the limitation as the direction of a free and intelligent agent to his proper interest, and prescribes no farther than is for the general good of those under that law: could they be happier without it, the law, as an useless thing, would of itself vanish; and that ill deserves the name of confinement which hedges us in only from bogs and precipices. So that, however it may be mistaken, the end of law is not to abolish or restrain, but to preserve and enlarge freedom: for in all the states of created beings capable of laws, where there is no law, there is no freedom: for liberty is, to be free from restraint and violence from others; which cannot be, where there is no law: but freedom is not, as we are told, a liberty for every man to do what he lists: (for who could be free, when every other man's humor[1] might domineer over him?) but a liberty to dispose, and order as he lists, his person, actions, possessions, and his whole property, within the allowance of those laws under which he is, and therein not to be subject to the arbitrary will of another, but freely follow his own.

§ 58. The power, then, that parents have over their children, arises from that duty which is incumbent on them, to take care of their offspring, during the imperfect state of childhood. To inform the mind, and govern the actions of their yet ignorant nonage,[2] till reason shall take its place, and ease them of that trouble, is what the children want, and the parents are bound to: for God having given man an understanding to direct his actions, has allowed him a freedom of will, and liberty of acting, as properly belonging thereunto, within the bounds of that law he is under. But while he is in an estate,[3] wherein he has not understanding of his own to direct his will, he is not to have any will of his own to follow: he that understands for him, must will for him too; he must prescribe to his will, and regulate his actions; but when

---

1 *humor* Temporary mood or state of mind.
2 *nonage* State of being immature, or under the age required for something.
3 *estate* Condition.

he comes to the estate that made his father a freeman, the son is a freeman too.

§ 59. This holds in all the laws a man is under, whether natural or civil. Is a man under the law of nature? What made him free of[1] that law? what gave him a free disposing of his property, according to his own will, within the compass of that law? I answer, a state of maturity wherein he might be supposed capable to know that law, that so he might keep his actions within the bounds of it. When he has acquired that state, he is presumed to know how far that law is to be his guide, and how far he may make use of his freedom, and so comes to have it; till then, some body else must guide him, who is presumed to know how far the law allows a liberty. If such a state of reason, such an age of discretion made him free, the same shall make his son free too. Is a man under the law of England? What made him free of that law? that is, to have the liberty to dispose of his actions and possessions according to his own will, within the permission of that law? A capacity of knowing that law; which is supposed by that law, at the age of one and twenty years, and in some cases sooner. If this made the father free, it shall make the son free too. Till then we see the law allows the son to have no will, but he is to be guided by the will of his father or guardian, who is to understand for him. And if the father die, and fail to substitute a deputy in his trust; if he has not provided a tutor, to govern his son, during his minority,[2] during his want of understanding, the law takes care to do it; some other must govern him, and be a will to him, till he has attained to a state of freedom, and his understanding be fit to take the government of his will. But after that, the father and son are equally free as much as tutor and pupil after nonage; equally subjects of the same law together, without any dominion left in the father over the life, liberty, or estate of his son, whether they be only in the state and under the law of nature, or under the positive laws of an established government.

§ 60. But if, through defects that may happen out of the ordinary course of nature, anyone comes not to such a degree of reason, wherein he might be supposed capable of knowing the law, and so living within the rules of it, he is never capable of being a free man, he is never let loose to the disposure[3] of his own will (because he knows no bounds to it, has not understanding, its proper guide) but is continued under the tuition and government of others, all the time his own understanding is incapable of that charge. And so lunatics and idiots are never set free from the government of their parents;

---

1   *of* Under.
2   *minority* Period during which a child is younger than the legal age of adulthood.
3   *disposure* Management.

Children, who are not as yet come unto those years whereat they
may have; and innocents which are excluded by a natural defect
from ever having; thirdly, madmen, which for the present cannot possibly have the use of right reason to guide themselves,
have for their guide, the reason that guideth other men which
are tutors over them, to seek and procure their good for them

says Hooker (*Ecclesiastical Polity Lib.* 1. § 7.). All which seems no
more than that duty, which God and nature has laid on man, as well as
other creatures, to preserve their offspring, till they can be able to shift
for themselves, and will scarce amount to an instance or proof of parents' regal authority.

§ 61. Thus we are born free, as we are born rational; not that we
have actually the exercise of either: age, that brings one, brings with
it the other too. And thus we see how natural freedom and subjection
to parents may consist together,[1] and are both founded on the same
principle. A child is free by his father's title, by his father's understanding, which is to govern him till he has it of his own. The freedom
of a man at years of discretion, and the subjection of a child to his parents, while yet short of that age, are so consistent, and so distinguish-
able, that the most blinded contenders for monarchy, by right of
fatherhood, cannot miss this difference; the most obstinate cannot but
allow their consistency: for were their doctrine all true, were the right
heir of Adam now known, and by that title settled a monarch in his
throne, invested with all the absolute unlimited power Sir Robert
Filmer talks of;[2] if he should die as soon as his heir were born, must
not the child, notwithstanding he were never so free, never so much
sovereign, be in subjection to his mother and nurse, to tutors and governors, till age and education brought him reason and ability to govern himself and others? The necessities of his life, the health of his
body, and the information of his mind, would require him to be directed by the will of others, and not his own; and yet will anyone think,
that this restraint and subjection were inconsistent with, or spoiled[3]
him of that liberty or sovereignty he had a right to, or gave away his
empire to those who had the government of his nonage? This govern-

---

1 *consist together*   Coexist.
2 *Sir Robert Filmer talks of*   Locke is dwelling on these matters at such length because Filmer's chief argument for the absolute power of the monarch is that the
   governing of society is based on the same principles as the governing of a family—that God granted Adam and his heirs (i.e., future monarchs) absolute fatherly authority over their people.
3 *spoiled*   Stripped.

ment over him only prepared him the better and sooner for it. If anybody should ask me, when my son is of age to be free? I shall answer, just when his monarch is of age to govern. "But at what time," says the judicious Hooker (*Eccl. Pol. Lib.* 1. sect. 6), "a man may be said to have attained so far forth the use of reason, as sufficeth to make him capable of those laws whereby he is then bound to guide his actions: this is a great deal more easy for sense to discern, than for anyone by skill and learning to determine."

§ 62. Commonwealths themselves take notice of, and allow, that there is a time when men are to begin to act like free men, and therefore till that time require not oaths of fealty,[1] or allegiance, or other public owning[2] of, or submission to the government of their countries.

§ 63. The freedom then of man, and liberty of acting according to his own will, is grounded on his having reason, which is able to instruct him in that law he is to govern himself by, and make him know how far he is left to the freedom of his own will. To turn him loose to an unrestrained liberty, before he has reason to guide him, is not the allowing him the privilege of his nature to be free; but to thrust him out among brutes, and abandon him to a state as wretched, and as much beneath that of a man, as theirs. This is that which puts the authority into the parents' hands to govern the minority of their children. God has made it their business to employ this care on their offspring, and has placed in them suitable inclinations of tenderness and concern to temper this power, to apply it, as his wisdom designed it, to the children's good, as long as they should need to be under it.

§ 64. But what reason can hence advance this care of the parents due to their offspring into an absolute arbitrary dominion of the father, whose power reaches no farther, than by such a discipline, as he finds most effectual, to give such strength and health to their bodies, such vigor and rectitude[3] to their minds, as may best fit his children to be most useful to themselves and others; and, if it be necessary to his condition, to make them work, when they are able, for their own subsistence. But in this power the mother too has her share with the father.

§ 65. Nay, this power so little belongs to the father by any peculiar right of nature, but only as he is guardian of his children, that when he quits his care of them, he loses his power over them, which goes along with their nourishment and education, to which it is inseparably annexed; and it belongs as much to the foster-father of an exposed

---

1   *fealty*   Loyalty, faithfulness; oaths of fealty were sworn by medieval vassals to their lords.
2   *owning*   Acknowledgment.
3   *rectitude*   Moral or intellectual correctness.

child,[1] as to the natural father of another. So little power does the bare act of begetting give a man over his issue; if all his care ends there, and this be all the title he has to the name and authority of a father. And what will become of this paternal power in that part of the world, where one woman has more than one husband at a time? or in those parts of America, where, when the husband and wife part, which happens frequently, the children are all left to the mother, follow her, and are wholly under her care and provision? If the father die while the children are young, do they not naturally every where owe the same obedience to their mother, during their minority, as to their father were he alive? and will anyone say, that the mother has a legislative power over her children? that she can make standing rules, which shall be of perpetual obligation, by which they ought to regulate all the concerns of their property, and bound their liberty all the course of their lives? or can she enforce the observation of them with capital punishments? for this is the proper power of the magistrate, of which the father has not so much as the shadow. His command over his children is but temporary, and reaches not their life or property: it is but a help to the weakness and imperfection of their nonage, a discipline necessary to their education: and though a father may dispose of his own possessions as he pleases, when his children are out of danger of perishing for want, yet his power extends not to the lives or goods, which either their own industry, or another's bounty has made theirs; nor to their liberty neither, when they are once arrived to the enfranchisement[2] of the years of discretion.[3] The father's empire then ceases, and he can from thence forwards no more dispose of the liberty of his son, than that of any other man: and it must be far from an absolute or perpetual jurisdiction, from which a man may withdraw himself, having license from divine authority to "leave father and mother, and cleave[4] to his wife."[5]

§ 66. But though there be a time when a child comes to be as free from subjection to the will and command of his father, as the father himself is free from subjection to the will of anybody else, and they are each under no other restraint, but that which is common to them both, whether it be the law of nature, or municipal law of their country; yet this freedom exempts not a son from that honor which he ought, by the

---

1   *exposed child*   Child who has been cast out or abandoned.
2   *enfranchisement*   Admission to political rights.
3   *years of discretion*   The time of life at which one is presumed to be capable of prudence and good judgment about one's actions; in English law, beginning at the age of fourteen.
4   *cleave*   Cling, join.
5   Matthew 19:5.

law of God and nature, to pay his parents. God having made the parents instruments in his great design of continuing the race of mankind, and the occasions of life to their children; as he has laid on them an obligation to nourish, preserve, and bring up their offspring; so he has laid on the children a perpetual obligation of honoring their parents, which containing in it an inward esteem and reverence to be shown by all outward expressions, ties up the child from any thing that may ever injure or affront, disturb or endanger, the happiness or life of those from whom he received his; and engages him in all actions of defense, relief, assistance and comfort of those, by whose means he entered into being, and has been made capable of any enjoyments of life: from this obligation no state, no freedom can absolve children. But this is very far from giving parents a power of command over their children, or an authority to make laws and dispose as they please of their lives or liberties. It is one thing to owe honor, respect, gratitude and assistance; another to require an absolute obedience and submission. The honor due to parents, a monarch in his throne owes his mother; and yet this lessens not his authority, nor subjects him to her government.

§ 67. The subjection of a minor places in the father a temporary government, which terminates with the minority of the child:[1] and the honor due from a child, places in the parents a perpetual right to respect, reverence, support and compliance too, more or less, as the father's care, cost, and kindness in his education, has been more or less. This ends not with minority, but holds in all parts and conditions of a man's life. The want of distinguishing these two powers, viz. that which the father has in the right of tuition,[2] during minority, and the right of honor all his life, may perhaps have caused a great part of the mistakes about this matter: for to speak properly of them, the first of these is rather the privilege of children, and duty of parents, than any prerogative[3] of paternal power. The nourishment and education of their children is a charge so incumbent on parents for their children's good, that nothing can absolve them from taking care of it: and though the power of commanding and chastising[4] them go along with it, yet God has woven into the principles of human nature such a tenderness for their offspring, that there is little fear that parents should use their power with too much rigor; the excess is seldom on the severe side, the strong bias of nature drawing the other way. And therefore God

---

1   *terminates with the minority of the child*   Ends when the child ceases to be a minor.
2   *tuition*   Teaching.
3   *prerogative*   Privilege restricted to certain people.
4   *chastising*   Scolding or punishing.

almighty when he would express his gentle dealing with the Israelites, he tells them, that though he chastened them, "he chastened them as a man chastens his son" (Deut. viii. 5), i.e., with tenderness and affection, and kept them under no severer discipline than what was absolutely best for them, and had been less kindness to have slackened. This is that power to which children are commanded obedience, that the pains and care of their parents may not be increased, or ill rewarded.

§ 68. On the other side, honor and support, all that which gratitude requires to return for the benefits received by and from them, is the indispensable duty of the child, and the proper privilege of the parents. This is intended for the parents' advantage, as the other is for the child's; though education, the parents' duty, seems to have most power, because the ignorance and infirmities of childhood stand in need of restraint and correction; which is a visible exercise of rule, and a kind of dominion. And that duty which is comprehended in the word "honor," requires less obedience, though the obligation be stronger on grown, than younger children: for who can think the command, "Children obey your parents," requires in a man, that has children of his own, the same submission to his father, as it does in his yet young children to him; and that by this precept he were bound to obey all his father's commands, if, out of a conceit of authority, he should have the indiscretion to treat him still as a boy?

§ 69. The first part then of paternal power, or rather duty, which is education, belongs so to the father, that it terminates at a certain season; when the business of education is over, it ceases of itself, and is also alienable[1] before: for a man may put the tuition of his son in other hands; and he that has made his son an apprentice to another, has discharged him, during that time, of a great part of his obedience both to himself and to his mother. But all the duty of honor, the other part, remains never the less entire to them; nothing can cancel that: it is so inseparable from them both, that the father's authority cannot dispossess the mother of this right, nor can any man discharge his son from honoring her that bore him. But both these are very far from a power to make laws, and enforcing them with penalties, that may reach estate, liberty, limbs and life. The power of commanding ends with nonage; and though, after that, honor and respect, support and defense, and whatsoever gratitude can oblige a man to, for the highest benefits he is naturally capable of, be always due from a son to his parents; yet

---

1 *alienable* Transferable away.

all this puts no scepter[1] into the father's hand, no sovereign power of commanding. He has no dominion over his son's property, or actions; nor any right, that his will should prescribe to his son's in all things; however it may become his·son in many things, not very inconvenient to him and his family, to pay a deference[2] to it.

§ 70. A man may owe honor and respect to an ancient, or wise man; defense to his child or friend; relief and support to the distressed; and gratitude to a benefactor, to such a degree, that all he has, all he can do, cannot sufficiently pay it: but all these give no authority, no right to anyone, of making laws over him from whom they are owing. And it is plain, all this is due not only to the bare title of father; not only because, as has been said, it is owing to the mother too; but because these obligations to parents, and the degrees of what is required of children, may be varied by the different care and kindness, trouble and expense, which is often employed upon one child more than another.

§ 71. This shows the reason how it comes to pass, that parents in societies, where they themselves are subjects, retain a power over their children, and have as much right to their subjection, as those who are in the state of nature. Which could not possibly be, if all political power were only paternal, and that in truth they were one and the same thing: for then, all paternal power being in the prince, the subject could naturally have none of it. But these two powers, political and paternal, are so perfectly distinct and separate; are built upon so different foundations, and given to so different ends, that every subject that is a father, has as much a paternal power over his children, as the prince has over his: and every prince, that has parents, owes them as much filial[3] duty and obedience, as the meanest of his subjects do to theirs; and can therefore contain not any part or degree of that kind of dominion, which a prince or magistrate has over his subject.

§ 72. Though the obligation on the parents to bring up their children, and the obligation on children to honor their parents, contain all the power on the one hand, and submission on the other, which are proper to this relation, yet there is another power ordinarily in the father, whereby he has a tie on the obedience of his children; which though it be common to him with other men, yet the occasions of showing it, almost constantly happening to fathers in their private families and in instances of it elsewhere being rare, and less taken notice of, it passes in the world for a part of "paternal jurisdiction." And this

---

1   *scepter*   Ceremonial staff, symbol of royal authority.
2   *become his son in many things ... to pay a deference*   Be proper or beneficial for the son in many ways to pay respect to his father's wishes.
3   *filial*   Of children to parents.

is the power men generally have to bestow their estates on those who please them best; the possession of the father being the expectation and inheritance of the children, ordinarily in certain proportions, according to the law and custom of each country; yet it is commonly in the father's power to bestow it with a more sparing or liberal hand, according as the behavior of this or that child has comported with[1] his will and humor.

§ 73. This is no small tie on the obedience of children: and there being always annexed to the enjoyment of land, a submission to the government of the country, of which that land is a part; it has been commonly supposed, that a father could oblige[2] his posterity to that government, of which he himself was a subject, and that his compact[3] held them; whereas, it being only a necessary condition annexed to the land, and the inheritance of an estate which is under that government, reaches only those who will take it on that condition, and so is no natural tie or engagement, but a voluntary submission: for every man's children being by nature as free as himself, or any of his ancestors ever were, may, while they are in that freedom, choose what society they will join themselves to, what commonwealth they will put themselves under. But if they will enjoy the inheritance of their ancestors, they must take it on the same terms their ancestors had it, and submit to all the conditions annexed to such a possession. By this power indeed fathers oblige their children to obedience to themselves, even when they are past minority, and most commonly too subject them to this or that political power: but neither of these by any peculiar right of fatherhood, but by the reward they have in their hands to enforce and recompense such a compliance; and is no more power than what a French man has over an English man, who by the hopes of an estate he will leave him, will certainly have a strong tie on his obedience: and if, when it is left him, he will enjoy it, he must certainly take it upon the conditions annexed to the possession of land in that country where it lies, whether it be France or England.

§ 74. To conclude then, though the father's power of commanding extends no farther than the minority of his children, and to a degree only fit for the discipline and government of that age; and though that honor and respect, and all that which the Latins called piety, which they indispensably owe to their parents all their lifetime, and in all es-

---

1 *has comported with* Was consistent with.
2 *oblige* Connect with bonds of loyalty or obligation.
3 *compact* Agreement. Locke here probably means that the father's tacit social contract with his government might be passed on to his child by inheritance of land.

tates, with all that support and defense is due to them, gives the father no power of governing, i.e., making laws and enacting penalties on his children; though by all this he has no dominion over the property or actions of his son: yet it is obvious to conceive how easy it was, in the first ages of the world, and in places still, where the thinness of people[1] gives families leave to separate into unpossessed quarters,[2] and they have room to remove or plant themselves in yet vacant habitations, for the father of the family to become the prince of[3] it; he had been a ruler from the beginning of the infancy of his children: and since without some government it would be hard for them to live together, it was likeliest it should, by the express or tacit consent of the children when they were grown up, be in the father, where it seemed without any change barely to continue; when indeed nothing more was required to it, than the permitting the father to exercise alone, in his family, that executive power of the law of nature, which every free man naturally has, and by that permission resigning up to him a monarchical power, while they remained in it. But that this was not by any paternal right, but only by the consent of his children, is evident from hence,[4] that nobody doubts, but[5] if a stranger, whom chance or business had brought to his family, had there killed any of his children, or committed any other fact,[6] he might condemn and put him to death, or otherwise have punished him, as well as any of his children; which it was impossible he should do by virtue of any paternal authority over one who was not his child, but by virtue of that executive power of

---

1   *thinness of people*   Low population density.

2   *unpossessed quarters*   Areas of unowned land.

3   *they have room ... the prince of*   [Locke's note] "It is no improbable opinion therefore, which the arch-philosopher [Aristotle—*Politics* books 3 and 4] was of, that the chief person in every household was always, as it were, a king: so when numbers of households joined themselves in civil societies together, kings were the first kind of governors among them, which is also, as it seemeth, the reason why the name of fathers continued still in them, who, of fathers, were made rulers; as also the ancient custom of governors to do as Melchizedec [Genesis 18.18-20], and being kings, to exercise the office of priests, which fathers did at the first, grew perhaps by the same occasion. Howbeit, this is not the only kind of regiment that has been received in the world. The inconveniencies of one kind have caused sundry others to be devised; so that in a word, all public regiment [rule], of what kind soever, seemeth evidently to have risen from the deliberate advice, consultation and composition between men, judging it convenient and behooveful [advantageous]; there being no impossibility in nature considered by itself, but that man might have lived without any public regiment" (Hooker, *Ecclesiastical Polity Lib*. 1. sect. 10).

4   *hence*   The following.

5   *but*   That.

6   *fact*   Evil deed.

the law of nature, which, as a man, he had a right to: and he alone could punish him in his family, where the respect of his children had laid by the exercise of such a power, to give way to the dignity and authority they were willing should remain in him, above the rest of his family.

§ 75. Thus it was easy, and almost natural for children, by a tacit, and scarce avoidable consent, to make way for the father's authority and government. They had been accustomed in their childhood to follow his direction, and to refer their little differences to him, and when they were men, who fitter to rule them? Their little properties, and less covetousness,[1] seldom afforded greater controversies; and when any should arise, where could they have a fitter umpire[2] than he, by whose care they had everyone been sustained and brought up, and who had a tenderness for them all? It is no wonder that they made no distinction betwixt minority and full age; nor looked after one and twenty, or any other age that might make them the free disposers of themselves and fortunes, when they could have no desire to be out of their pupilage:[3] the government they had been under, during it, continued still to be more their protection than restraint; and they could no where find a greater security to their peace, liberties, and fortunes, than in the rule of a father.

§ 76. Thus the natural fathers of families, by an insensible change, became the politic[4] monarchs of them too: and as they chanced to live long, and leave able and worthy heirs, for several successions, or otherwise; so they laid the foundations of hereditary, or elective kingdoms, under several constitutions and manners, according as chance, contrivance, or occasions happened to mold them. But if princes have their titles in their fathers' right, and it be a sufficient proof of the natural right of fathers to political authority, because they commonly were those in whose hands we find, de facto,[5] the exercise of government: I say, if this argument be good, it will as strongly prove, that all princes, nay princes only, ought to be priests, since it is as certain, that in the beginning, the father of the family was priest, as that he was ruler in his own household.

---

1 *covetousness* Desire to possess others' property.
2 *umpire* Arbitrator.
3 *pupilage* Period of being a young student.
4 *politic* Political.
5 *de facto* Latin: in fact (contrasted here with Latin: *de jure* or "by law").

Chapter 7. Of Political or Civil Society

§ 77. God having made man such a creature, that in his own judgment, it was not good for him to be alone, put him under strong obligations of necessity, convenience, and inclination to drive him into society, as well as fitted him with understanding and language to continue and enjoy it. The first society was between man and wife, which gave beginning to that between parents and children; to which, in time, that between master and servant came to be added: and though all these might, and commonly did meet together, and make up but one family,[1] wherein the master or mistress of it had some sort of rule proper to a family; each of these, or all together, came short of political society, as we shall see, if we consider the different ends, ties, and bounds of each of these.

§ 78. Conjugal[2] society is made by a voluntary compact between man and woman; and though it consist chiefly in such a communion[3] and right in one another's bodies as is necessary to its chief end, procreation; yet it draws with it mutual support and assistance, and a communion of interests too, as necessary not only to unite their care and affection, but also necessary to their common off-spring, who have a right to be nourished, and maintained by them, till they are able to provide for themselves.

§ 79. For the end of conjunction, between male and female, being not barely procreation, but the continuation of the species; this conjunction betwixt male and female ought to last, even after procreation, so long as is necessary to the nourishment and support of the young ones, who are to be sustained by those that got them, till they are able to shift and provide for themselves. This rule, which the infinite wise maker has set to the works of his hands, we find the inferior creatures steadily obey. In those viviparous[4] animals which feed on grass, the conjunction between male and female lasts no longer than the very act of copulation; because the teat of the dam[5] being sufficient to nourish the young, till it be able to feed on grass, the male only begets,[6] but concerns not himself for the female or young, to whose sustenance he can contribute nothing. But in beasts of prey the conjunction lasts

---

1 *family*   Household.
2 *Conjugal*   Relating to marriage.
3 *communion*   Intimate connection.
4 *viviparous*   Live-bearing (as contrasted with egg-laying).
5 *dam*   Female parent.
6 *begets*   Impregnates the female.

longer: because the dam not being able well to subsist herself, and nourish her numerous off-spring by her own prey alone, a more laborious, as well as more dangerous way of living, than by feeding on grass, the assistance of the male is necessary to the maintenance of their common family, which cannot subsist till they are able to prey for themselves, but by the joint care of male and female. The same is to be observed in all birds, (except some domestic ones, where plenty of food excuses the cock from feeding, and taking care of the young brood) whose young needing food in the nest, the cock and hen continue mates, till the young are able to use their wing, and provide for themselves.

§ 80. And herein I think lies the chief, if not the only reason, why the male and female in mankind are tied to a longer conjunction than other creatures, viz. because the female is capable of conceiving, and de facto is commonly with child again, and brings forth too a new birth, long before the former is out of a dependency for support on his parents' help, and able to shift for himself, and has all the assistance is due to him from his parents: whereby the father, who is bound to take care for those he has begot, is under an obligation to continue in conjugal society with the same woman longer than other creatures, whose young being able to subsist of themselves, before the time of procreation returns again, the conjugal bond dissolves of itself, and they are at liberty, till Hymen[1] at his usual anniversary season summons them again to choose new mates. Wherein one cannot but admire the wisdom of the great Creator, who having given to man foresight, and an ability to lay up for the future, as well as to supply the present necessity, has made it necessary, that society of man and wife should be more lasting, than of male and female among other creatures; that so their industry might be encouraged, and their interest better united, to make provision and lay up goods for their common issue, which uncertain mixture, or easy and frequent solutions of conjugal society would mightily disturb.

§ 81. But though these are ties upon mankind, which make the conjugal bonds more firm and lasting in man, than the other species of animals; yet it would give one reason to enquire, why this compact, where procreation and education are secured, and inheritance taken care for, may not be made determinable,[2] either by consent, or at a certain time, or upon certain conditions, as well as any other voluntary compacts, there being no necessity in the nature of the thing, nor to the ends of it, that it should always be for life; I mean, to such as are under

---

1 *Hymen* Greek god of marriage.
2 *determinable* Able to be ended.

no restraint of any positive law, which ordains all such contracts to be perpetual.

§ 82. But the husband and wife, though they have but one common concern, yet having different understandings, will unavoidably sometimes have different wills too; it therefore being necessary that the last determination,[1] i.e., the rule, should be placed somewhere; it naturally falls to the man's share, as the abler and the stronger. But this reaching but to the things of their common interest and property,[2] leaves the wife in the full and free possession of what by contract is her peculiar right,[3] and gives the husband no more power over her life than she has over his; the power of the husband being so far from that of an absolute monarch, that the wife has in many cases a liberty to separate from him, where natural right, or their contract allows it; whether that contract be made by themselves in the state of nature, or by the customs or laws of the country they live in; and the children upon such separation fall to the father or mother's lot, as such contract does determine.

§ 83. For all the ends of marriage being to be obtained under politic government, as well as in the state of nature, the civil magistrate does not abridge the right or power of either naturally necessary to those ends, viz. procreation and mutual support and assistance while they are together; but only decides any controversy that may arise between man and wife about them. If it were otherwise, and that absolute sovereignty and power of life and death naturally belonged to the husband, and were necessary to the society between man and wife, there could be no matrimony in any of those countries where the husband is allowed no such absolute authority. But the ends of matrimony requiring no such power in the husband, the condition of conjugal society put it not in him, it being not at all necessary to that state. Conjugal society could subsist and attain its ends without it; nay, community of goods, and the power over them, mutual assistance and maintenance, and other things belonging to conjugal society, might be varied and regulated by that contract which unites man and wife in that society, as far as may consist with procreation and the bringing up of children till they could shift for themselves; nothing being necessary to any society, that is not necessary to the ends for which it is made.

§ 84. The society betwixt parents and children, and the distinct rights and powers belonging respectively to them, I have treated of so

---

1   *last determination*   The final say in the matter.
2   *But this reaching ... property*   But since this extends only to what is their common interest and property.
3   *peculiar right*   Private property.

largely, in the foregoing chapter, that I shall not here need to say any thing of it. And I think it is plain, that it is far different from a politic society.

§ 85. Master and servant are names as old as history, but given to those of far different condition; for a freeman makes himself a servant to another, by selling him, for a certain time, the service he undertakes to do, in exchange for wages he is to receive: and though this commonly puts him into the family of his master, and under the ordinary discipline thereof; yet it gives the master but a temporary power over him, and no greater than what is contained in the contract between them. But there is another sort of servants, which by a peculiar name[1] we call slaves, who being captives taken in a just war, are by the right of nature subjected to the absolute dominion and arbitrary power of their masters. These men having, as I say, forfeited their lives, and with it their liberties, and lost their estates; and being in the state of slavery, not capable of any property, cannot in that state be considered as any part of civil society; the chief end whereof is the preservation of property.

§ 86. Let us therefore consider a master of a family with all these subordinate relations of wife, children, servants, and slaves, united under the domestic rule of a family; which, whatever resemblance it may have in its order, offices, and number too, with a little commonwealth, yet is very far from it, both in its constitution, power and end: or if it must be thought a monarchy, and the paterfamilias[2] the absolute monarch in it, absolute monarchy will have but a very shattered and short power, when it is plain, by what has been said before, that the master of the family has a very distinct and differently limited power, both as to time and extent, over those several persons that are in it; for excepting the slave (and the family is as much a family, and his power as paterfamilias as great, whether there be any slaves in his family or no) he has no legislative power of life and death over any of them, and none too but[3] what a mistress of a family may have as well as he. And he certainly can have no absolute power over the whole family, who has but a very limited one over every individual in it. But how a family, or any other society of men, differ from that which is properly political society, we shall best see, by considering wherein political society itself consists.

§ 87. Man being born, as has been proved, with a title to perfect freedom, and an uncontrolled enjoyment of all the rights and privi-

---

1 *by a peculiar name* Using a distinctive name applicable to them alone.
2 *paterfamilias* Literally "father of the family," but with the implication of complete authority.
3 *none too but* Nothing but.

leges of the law of nature, equally with any other man, or number of men in the world, has by nature a power, not only to preserve his property, that is, his life, liberty and estate, against the injuries and attempts of other men; but to judge of, and punish the breaches of that law in others, as he is persuaded the offence deserves, even with death itself, in crimes where the heinousness of the fact,[1] in his opinion, requires it. But because no political society can be, nor subsist, without having in itself the power to preserve the property, and in order thereunto, punish the offences of all those of that society; there, and there only is political society, where everyone of the members has quitted this natural power, resigned[2] it up into the hands of the community in all cases that exclude him not from appealing for protection to the law established by it. And thus all private judgment of every particular member being excluded, the community comes to be umpire, by settled standing rules, indifferent, and the same to all parties; and by men having authority from the community, for the execution of those rules, decides all the differences that may happen between any members of that society concerning any matter of right; and punishes those offences which any member has committed against the society, with such penalties as the law has established: whereby it is easy to discern, who are, and who are not, in political society together. Those who are united into one body, and have a common established law and judicature[3] to appeal to, with authority to decide controversies between them, and punish offenders, are in civil society one with another: but those who have no such common appeal, I mean on earth, are still in the state of nature, each being, where there is no other, judge for himself, and executioner; which is, as I have before shown it, the perfect state of nature.

§ 88. And thus the commonwealth comes by a power to set down what punishment shall belong to the several transgressions which they think worthy of it, committed among the members of that society, (which is the power of making laws) as well as it has the power to punish any injury done unto any of its members, by anyone that is not of it, (which is the power of war and peace;) and all this for the preservation of the property of all the members of that society, as far as is possible. But though every man who has entered into civil society, and is become a member of any commonwealth, has thereby quitted his power to punish offences, against the law of nature, in prosecution[4] of

---

1   *heinousness of the fact*   Evil nature of the horrible deed.
2   *resigned*   Relinquished claim to.
3   *judicature*   System for administration of justice.
4   *prosecution*   Pursuit, as if in court, of legal action.

his own private judgment, yet with the judgment of offences, which he has given up to the legislative in all cases, where he can appeal to the magistrate, he has given a right to the commonwealth to employ his force, for the execution of the judgments of the commonwealth, whenever he shall be called to it; which indeed are his own judgments, they being made by himself, or his representative. And herein we have the original of the legislative and executive power of civil society, which is to judge by standing laws, how far offences are to be punished, when committed within the commonwealth; and also to determine, by occasional[1] judgments founded on the present circumstances of the fact, how far injuries from without[2] are to be vindicated;[3] and in both these to employ all the force of all the members, when there shall be need.

§ 89. Wherever therefore any number of men are so united into one society, as to quit everyone his executive power of the law of nature, and to resign it to the public, there and there only is a political, or civil society. And this is done, wherever any number of men, in the state of nature, enter into society to make one people, one body politic, under one supreme government; or else when anyone joins himself to, and incorporates with any government already made: for hereby he authorizes the society, or which is all one, the legislative thereof, to make laws for him, as the public good of the society shall require; to the execution whereof, his own assistance (as to his own decrees) is due. And this puts men out of a state of nature into that of a commonwealth, by setting up a judge on earth, with authority to determine all the controversies, and redress the injuries that may happen to any member of the commonwealth; which judge is the legislative, or magistrates appointed by it. And wherever there are any number of men, however associated, that have no such decisive power to appeal to, there they are still in the state of nature.

§ 90. Hence it is evident, that absolute monarchy, which by some men is counted the only government in the world, is indeed inconsistent with civil society, and so can be no form of civil government at all: for the end of civil society, being to avoid, and remedy those inconveniencies of the state of nature, which necessarily follow from every man's being judge in his own case, by setting up a known authority, to which everyone of that society may appeal upon any injury received, or controversy that may arise, and which everyone of the society ought

---

1 *occasional* Specific to the occasion.
2 *without* Outside.
3 *vindicated* Punished.

to obey;[1] where-ever any persons are, who have not such an authority to appeal to, for the decision of any difference between them, there those persons are still in the state of nature; and so is every absolute prince, in respect of those who are under his dominion.

§ 91. For he being supposed to have all, both legislative and executive power in himself alone, there is no judge to be found, no appeal lies open to anyone, who may fairly, and indifferently, and with authority decide, and from whose decision relief and redress may be expected of any injury or inconveniency, that may be suffered from the prince, or by his order: so that such a man, however entitled, "Czar," or "Grand Seignior," or how you please, is as much in the state of nature, with all under his dominion, as he is with the rest of mankind: for wherever any two men are, who have no standing rule, and common judge to appeal to on earth, for the determination of controversies of right betwixt them, there they are still in the state of nature, and under all the inconveniencies of it, with only this woeful difference to the subject, or rather slave of an absolute prince:[2] that whereas, in the ordinary state of nature, he has a liberty to judge of his right, and according to the best of his power, to maintain it; now, whenever his property is invaded by the will and order of his monarch, he has not only no appeal, as those in society ought to have, but as if he were degraded from the common state of rational creatures, is denied a lib-

---

1 *for the end of civil society ... society ought to obey* [Locke's note] "The public
  power of all society is above every soul contained in the same society; and the
  principal use of that power is, to give laws unto all that are under it, which laws
  in such cases we must obey, unless there be reason shown which may necessarily
  enforce [unavoidably give strength to the idea], that the law of reason, or of God,
  doth enjoin [impose] the contrary" (Hooker, *Ecclesiastical Polity Lib.* I. sect. 16).

2 *for wherever any two men ... an absolute prince* [Locke's note] "To take away
  all such mutual grievances, injuries and wrongs," i.e., such as attend men in the
  state of nature, "there was no way but only by growing into composition and
  agreement among themselves, by ordaining some kind of government public, and
  by yielding themselves subject thereunto, that unto whom they granted authority
  to rule and govern, by them the peace, tranquility and happy estate of the rest
  might be procured. Men always knew that where force and injury was offered,
  they might be defenders of themselves; they knew that however men may seek
  their own commodity [advantage], yet if this were done with injury unto others,
  it was not to be suffered, but by all men, and all good means to be withstood. Finally, they knew that no man might in reason take upon him to determine his
  own right, and according to his own determination proceed in maintenance
  thereof, in as much as every man is towards himself, and them whom he greatly
  affects, partial; and therefore that strifes and troubles would be endless, except
  they gave their common consent, all to be ordered by some, whom they should
  agree upon, without which consent there would be no reason that one man should
  take upon him to be lord or judge over another" (Hooker, *Ecclesiastical Polity
  Lib.* I. sect. 10).

erty to judge of, or to defend his right; and so is exposed to all the misery and inconveniencies, that a man can fear from one, who being in the unrestrained state of nature, is yet corrupted with flattery, and armed with power.

§ 92. For he that thinks absolute power purifies men's blood, and corrects the baseness of human nature, need read but the history of this, or any other age, to be convinced of the contrary. He that would have been insolent and injurious in the woods of America, would not probably be much better in a throne; where perhaps learning and religion shall be found out to justify all that he shall do to his subjects, and the sword presently silence all those that dare question it: for what the protection of absolute monarchy is, what kind of fathers of their countries it makes princes to be and to what a degree of happiness and security it carries civil society, where this sort of government is grown to perfection, he that will look into the late relation of Ceylon,[1] may easily see.

§ 93. In absolute monarchies indeed, as well as other governments of the world, the subjects have an appeal to the law, and judges to decide any controversies, and restrain any violence that may happen betwixt the subjects themselves, one among another. This everyone thinks necessary, and believes he deserves to be thought a declared enemy to society and mankind, who should go about to take it away. But whether this be from a true love of mankind and society, and such a charity as we owe all one to another, there is reason to doubt: for this is no more than what every man, who loves his own power, profit, or greatness, may and naturally must do, keep those animals from hurting, or destroying one another, who labor and drudge only for his pleasure and advantage; and so are taken care of, not out of any love the master has for them, but love of himself, and the profit they bring him: for if it be asked, what security, what fence is there, in such a state, against the violence and oppression of this absolute ruler? the very question can scarce be borne. They are ready to tell you, that it deserves death only to ask after safety. Betwixt subject and subject, they will grant, there must be measures, laws and judges, for their mutual peace and security: but as for the ruler, he ought to be absolute, and is above all such circumstances; because he has power to do more hurt and wrong, it is right when he does it. To ask how you may be guarded from harm, or injury, on that side where the strongest hand is to do it, is presently the voice of faction and rebellion: as if when men quitting

---

1 *the late relation of Ceylon* Robert Knox, *Historical Relation of Ceylon* (1681); this was, at the time, a very well-known autobiographical account of a sailor who was held captive by a king of Ceylon—now Sri Lanka—for nineteen years.

the state of nature entered into society, they agreed that all of them but one, should be under the restraint of laws, but that he should still retain all the liberty of the state of nature, increased with power, and made licentious by impunity.[1] This is to think, that men are so foolish, that they take care to avoid what mischiefs may be done them by polecats, or foxes; but are content, nay, think it safety, to be devoured by lions.

§ 94. But whatever flatterers may talk to amuse people's understandings, it hinders not men from feeling; and when they perceive, that any man, in whatever station, is out of the bounds of the civil society which they are of, and that they have no appeal on earth against any harm, they may receive from him, they are apt to think themselves in the state of nature, in respect of him whom they find to be so; and to take care, as soon as they can, to have that safety and security in civil society, for which it was first instituted, and for which only they entered into it. And therefore, though perhaps at first, (as shall be shown more at large hereafter in the following part of this discourse) some one good and excellent man having got a preeminence among the rest, had this deference paid to his goodness and virtue, as to a kind of natural authority, that the chief rule, with arbitration of their differences, by a tacit consent devolved[2] into his hands, without any other caution, but the assurance they had of his uprightness and wisdom; yet when time, giving authority, and (as some men would persuade us) sacredness of customs, which the negligent, and unforeseeing innocence of the first ages began, had brought in successors of another stamp,[3] the people finding their properties not secure under the government, as then it was, (whereas government has no other end but the preservation of[4] property) could never be safe nor at rest, nor think themselves in civil society, till the legislature was placed in collective bodies of men, call them senate, parliament, or what you please. By which

---

1   *made licentious by impunity*   Made immoral by freedom from consequences of their actions.
2   *devolved*   Passed into.
3   *stamp*   Type.
4   *no other end but the preservation of*   [Locke's note] "At the first, when some certain kind of regiment was once appointed, it may be that nothing was then farther thought upon for the manner of governing, but all permitted unto their wisdom and discretion, which were to rule, till by experience they found this for all parts very inconvenient, so as the thing which they had devised for a remedy, did indeed but increase the sore, which it should have cured. They saw, that to live by one man's will, became the cause of all men's misery. This constrained them to come unto laws, wherein all men might see their duty beforehand, and know the penalties of transgressing them" (Hooker, *Ecclesiastical Polity Lib.* I. sect. 10).

means every single person became subject, equally with other the meanest men,[1] to those laws, which he himself, as part of the legislative, had established; nor could anyone, by his own authority; avoid the force of the law, when once made; nor by any pretence of superiority plead exemption, thereby to license his own, or the miscarriages[2] of any of his dependents.[3] No man in civil society can be exempted from the laws of it: for if any man may do what he thinks fit, and there be no appeal on earth, for redress or security against any harm he shall do; I ask, whether he be not perfectly still in the state of nature, and so can be no part or member of that civil society; unless anyone will say, the state of nature and civil society are one and the same thing, which I have never yet found anyone so great a patron of anarchy as to affirm.

Chapter 8. Of the Beginning of Political Societies

§ 95. Men being, as has been said, by nature, all free, equal, and independent, no one can be put out of this estate, and subjected to the political power of another, without his own consent. The only way whereby anyone divests himself of his natural liberty, and puts on the bonds of civil society, is by agreeing with other men to join and unite into a community for their comfortable, safe, and peaceable living one among another, in a secure enjoyment of their properties, and a greater security against any, that are not of it. This any number of men may do, because it injures not the freedom of the rest; they are left as they were in the liberty of the state of nature. When any number of men have so consented to make one community or government, they are thereby presently incorporated, and make one body politic, wherein the majority have a right to act and conclude[4] the rest.

§ 96. For when any number of men have, by the consent of every individual, made a community, they have thereby made that community one body, with a power to act as one body, which is only by the will and determination of the majority: for that which acts[5] any community, being only the consent of the individuals of it, and it being necessary to that which is one body to move one way; it is necessary the body should move that way whither the greater force carries it, which is the consent of the majority: or else it is impossible it should act or continue one body, one community, which the consent of every

---

1 *other the meanest men* Other people of the lowest social status.
2 *miscarriages* Mishandlings.
3 *dependents* [Locke's note] "Civil law being the act of the whole body politic, doth therefore overrule each several part of the same body" (Hooker, *Ibid.*).
4 *conclude* Decide for.
5 *acts* Puts in motion.

individual that united into it, agreed that it should; and so everyone is bound by that consent to be concluded by the majority. And therefore we see, that in assemblies, empowered to act by positive laws, where no number is set by that positive law which empowers them, the act of the majority passes for the act of the whole, and of course determines, as having, by the law of nature and reason, the power of the whole.

§ 97. And thus every man, by consenting with others to make one body politic under one government, puts himself under an obligation, to everyone of that society, to submit to the determination of the majority, and to be concluded by it; or else this original compact, whereby he with others incorporates into one society, would signify nothing, and be no compact, if he be left free, and under no other ties than he was in before in the state of nature. For what appearance would there be of any compact? what new engagement if he were no farther tied by any decrees of the society, than he himself thought fit, and did actually consent to? This would be still as great a liberty, as he himself had before his compact, or anyone else in the state of nature has, who may submit himself, and consent to any acts of it if he thinks fit.

§ 98. For if the consent of the majority shall not, in reason, be received as the act of the whole, and conclude every individual; nothing but the consent of every individual can make any thing to be the act of the whole: but such a consent is next to impossible ever to be had, if we consider the infirmities of health, and avocations[1] of business, which in a number, though much less than that of a commonwealth, will necessarily keep many away from the public assembly. To which if we add the variety of opinions, and contrariety of interests, which unavoidably happen in all collections of men, the coming into society upon such terms would be only like Cato's coming into the theatre, only to go out again.[2] Such a constitution as this would make the mighty Leviathan[3] of a shorter duration, than the feeblest creatures, and not let it outlast the day it was born in: which cannot be supposed, till we can think, that rational creatures should desire and constitute so-

---

1   *avocations*   Distractions.
2   *Cato's coming ... go out again*   Marcus Porcius Cato Uticensis (95-46 BCE), also known as Cato the Younger, was a Roman statesman and orator known for his emphasis on moral integrity. In one of his *Epigrams*, the Roman poet Martial implies that Cato's very presence would be an unwelcome distraction in the lighthearted context of the theatre: "Why, stern Cato, did you come to the theatre? Did you then enter only to leave?"
3   *Leviathan*   A large beast or sea-monster in the Bible. The reference here is to Hobbes, who used that term as the title of his famous book and as a name for the huge and formidable state with absolute powers that he advocated as the only effective form of government. Locke was eager to disassociate himself from Hobbes; this is one of the very few more-or-less explicit references to him.

cieties only to be dissolved: for where the majority cannot conclude the rest, there they cannot act as one body, and consequently will be immediately dissolved again.

§ 99. Whosoever therefore out of a state of nature unite into a community, must be understood to give up all the power, necessary to the ends for which they unite into society, to the majority of the community, unless they expressly agreed in any number greater than the majority. And this is done by barely agreeing to unite into one political society, which is all the compact that is, or needs be, between the individuals, that enter into, or make up a commonwealth. And thus that, which begins and actually constitutes any political society, is nothing but the consent of any number of freemen capable of a majority to unite and incorporate into such a society. And this is that, and that only, which did, or could give beginning to any lawful government in the world.

§ 100. To this I find two objections made.

First, That there are no instances to be found in story,[1] of a company of men independent, and equal one among another, that met together, and in this way began and set up a government.

Secondly, It is impossible of right, that men should do so, because all men being born under government, they are to submit to that, and are not at liberty to begin a new one.

§ 101. To the first there is this to answer, That it is not at all to be wondered, that history gives us but a very little account of men, that lived together in the state of nature. The inconveniencies of that condition, and the love and want of society, no sooner brought any number of them together, but they presently united and incorporated, if they designed to continue together. And if we may not suppose men ever to have been in the state of nature, because we hear not much of them in such a state, we may as well suppose the armies of Salmanasser[2] or Xerxes[3] were never children, because we hear little of them, till they were men, and embodied in armies. Government is every where antecedent to records, and letters seldom come in among a people till a long continuation of civil society has, by other more necessary arts, provided for their safety, ease, and plenty: and then they begin to look after the history of their founders, and search into their original, when they have outlived the memory of it: for it is with commonwealths as with particular persons, they are commonly igno-

---

1 *story* history.
2 *Salmanasser* Shalmaneser V (or IV) (727-722 BCE) was king of Assyria; his fight against the Israelites is referred to in the Bible (2 Kings).
3 *Xerxes* Xerxes (d. 465 BCE) was king of Persia; he led the second Persian invasion of Greece.

rant of their own births and infancies: and if they know any thing of their original, they are beholden for it, to the accidental records that others have kept of it. And those that we have, of the beginning of any polities in the world, excepting that of the Jews, where God himself immediately interposed, and which favors not at all paternal dominion, are all either plain instances of such a beginning as I have mentioned, or at least have manifest footsteps of it.

§ 102. He must show a strange inclination to deny evident matter of fact, when it agrees not with his hypothesis, who will not allow, that the beginning of Rome and Venice were by the uniting together of several men free and independent one of another, among whom there was no natural superiority or subjection. And if Josephus Acosta's word may be taken, he tells us, that in many parts of America there was no government at all. "There are great and apparent conjectures," says he, "that these men," speaking of those of Peru, "for a long time had neither kings nor commonwealths, but lived in troops, as they do this day in Florida, the Cheriquanas, those of Brazil, and many other nations, which have no certain kings, but as occasion is offered, in peace or war, they choose their captains as they please." 1.1. c. 25.[1] If it be said, that every man there was born subject to his father, or the head of his family; that the subjection due from a child to a father took not away his freedom of uniting into what political society he thought fit, has been already proved. But be that as it will, these men, it is evident, were actually free; and whatever superiority some politicians now would place in any of them, they themselves claimed it not, but by consent were all equal, till by the same consent they set rulers over themselves. So that their politic societies all began from a voluntary union, and the mutual agreement of men freely acting in the choice of their governors, and forms of government.

§ 103. And I hope those who went away from Sparta with Palantus, mentioned by Justin, 1. 3. c. 4.[2] will be allowed to have been freemen independent one of another, and to have set up a government over themselves, by their own consent. Thus I have given several examples, out of history, of people free and in the state of nature, that being met together incorporated and began a commonwealth. And if the want

---

1   *1.1. c. 25*   In *Natural and Moral History of the Indies* by José de Acosta (Spanish, 1540-1600). Acosta's book provided the first detailed description of the geography and culture of Latin America and of Aztec history.

2   *those who went ... Justin, 1. 3. c. 4*   Marcus Junianus Justinus, Roman historian of the third century CE. In his major work (now lost) he described the group of young Spartans, who, born out of wedlock and thus denied rights in Sparta, left and, under their leader Phalanthus, conquered Tarentum (modern Taranto) in Southern Italy around 708 BCE and set up a new independent state.

of such instances be an argument to prove that government were not, nor could not be so begun, I suppose the contenders for paternal empire were better let it alone, than urge it against natural liberty: for if they can give so many instances, out of history, of governments begun upon paternal right, I think (though at best an argument from what has been, to what should of right be, has no great force) one might, without any great danger, yield them the cause. But if I might advise them in the case, they would do well not to search too much into the original of governments, as they have begun de facto, lest they should find, at the foundation of most of them, something very little favorable to the design they promote, and such a power as they contend for.

§ 104. But to conclude, reason being plain on our side, that men are naturally free, and the examples of history showing, that the governments of the world, that were begun in peace, had their beginning laid on that foundation, and were made by the consent of the people; there can be little room for doubt, either where the right is, or what has been the opinion, or practice of mankind, about the first erecting of governments.

§ 105. I will not deny, that if we look back as far as history will direct us, towards the original of commonwealths, we shall generally find them under the government and administration of one man. And I am also apt to believe, that where a family was numerous enough to subsist by itself, and continued entire together, without mixing with others, as it often happens, where there is much land, and few people, the government commonly began in the father: for the father having, by the law of nature, the same power with every man else to punish, as he thought fit, any offences against that law, might thereby punish his transgressing children, even when they were men, and out of their pupilage;[1] and they were very likely to submit to his punishment, and all join with him against the offender, in their turns, giving him thereby power to execute his sentence against any transgression, and so in effect make him the law-maker, and governor over all that remained in conjunction with his family. He was fittest to be trusted; paternal affection secured their property and interest under his care; and the custom of obeying him, in their childhood, made it easier to submit to him, rather than to any other. If therefore they must have one to rule them, as government is hardly to be avoided among men that live together; who so likely to be the man as he that was their common father; unless negligence, cruelty, or any other defect of mind or body made him unfit for it? But when either the father died, and left his next heir, for want of age, wisdom, courage, or any other qualities, less fit

---

1   *out of their pupilage*   No longer school-age.

for rule; or where several families met, and consented to continue together; there, it is not to be doubted, but they used their natural freedom, to set up him, whom they judged the ablest, and most likely, to rule well over them. Conformable hereunto we find the people of America, who (living out of the reach of the conquering swords, and spreading domination of the two great empires of Peru and Mexico) enjoyed their own natural freedom, though, caeteris paribus,[1] they commonly prefer the heir of their deceased king; yet if they find him any way weak, or incapable, they pass him by, and set up the stoutest and bravest man for their ruler.

§ 106. Thus, though looking back as far as records give us any account of peopling the world, and the history of nations, we commonly find the government to be in one hand; yet it destroys not that which I affirm, viz. that the beginning of politic society depends upon the consent of the individuals, to join into, and make one society; who, when they are thus incorporated, might set up what form of government they thought fit. But this having given occasion to men to mistake, and think, that by nature government was monarchical, and belonged to the father, it may not be amiss here to consider, why people in the beginning generally pitched upon[2] this form, which though perhaps the father's pre-eminency might, in the first institution of some commonwealths, give a rise to, and place in the beginning, the power in one hand; yet it is plain that the reason, that continued the form of government in a single person, was not any regard, or respect to paternal authority; since all petty monarchies, that is, almost all monarchies, near their original, have been commonly, at least upon occasion, elective.

§ 107. First then, in the beginning of things, the father's government of the childhood of those sprung from him, having accustomed them to the rule of one man, and taught them that where it was exercised with care and skill, with affection and love to those under it, it was sufficient to procure and preserve to men all the political happiness they sought for in society. It was no wonder that they should pitch upon, and naturally run into that form of government, which from their infancy they had been all accustomed to; and which, by experience, they had found both easy and safe. To which, if we add, that monarchy being simple, and most obvious to men, whom neither experience had instructed in forms of government, nor the ambition or insolence of empire had taught to beware of the encroachments[3] of prerogative,

---

1 *caeteris paribus* Latin: everything else being equal.
2 *pitched upon* Settled on.
3 *encroachments* Illicit inroads.

or the inconveniencies of absolute power, which monarchy in succession was apt to lay claim to, and bring upon them, it was not at all strange, that they should not much trouble themselves to think of methods of restraining any exorbitances[1] of those to whom they had given the authority over them, and of balancing the power of government, by placing several parts of it in different hands. They had neither felt the oppression of tyrannical dominion, nor did the fashion of the age, nor their possessions, or way of living, (which afforded little matter for covetousness or ambition) give them any reason to apprehend[2] or provide against it; and therefore it is no wonder they put themselves into such a frame of government, as was not only, as I said, most obvious and simple, but also best suited to their present state and condition; which stood more in need of defense against foreign invasions and injuries, than of multiplicity of laws. The equality of a simple poor way of living, confining their desires within the narrow bounds of each man's small property, made few controversies,[3] and so no need of many laws to decide them, or variety of officers to superintend the process, or look after the execution of justice, where there were but few trespasses, and few offenders. Since then those, who like one another so well as to join into society, cannot but be supposed to have some acquaintance and friendship together, and some trust one in another; they could not but have greater apprehensions of others, than of one another: and therefore their first care and thought cannot but be supposed to be, how to secure themselves against foreign force. It was natural for them to put themselves under a frame of government which might best serve to that end, and choose the wisest and bravest man to conduct them in their wars, and lead them out against their enemies, and in this chiefly be their ruler.

§ 108. Thus we see, that the kings of the Indians in America, which is still a pattern of the first ages in Asia and Europe, while the inhabitants were too few for the country, and want of people and money gave men no temptation to enlarge their possessions of land, or contest for wider extent of ground, are little more than generals of their armies; and though they command absolutely in war, yet at home and in time of peace they exercise very little dominion, and have but a very moderate sovereignty, the resolutions of peace and war being ordinarily either in the people, or in a council. Though the war itself, which admits not of plurality of governors, naturally devolves the command into the king's sole authority.

---

1 *exorbitances*   Unreasonable extremes.
2 *apprehend*   Fear.
3 *controversies*   Disputes.

§ 109. And thus in Israel itself, the chief business of their judges, and first kings, seems to have been to be captains in war, and leaders of their armies; which (besides what is signified by "going out and in before the people," which was, to march forth to war, and home again in the heads of their forces) appears plainly in the story of Jephtha. The Ammonites making war upon Israel, the Gileadites in fear send to Jephtha, a bastard of their family whom they had cast off, and article with him, if he will assist them against the Ammonites, to make him their ruler; which they do in these words, "And the people made him head and captain over them" (Judges 11.11), which was, as it seems, all one as to be judge. "And he judged Israel" (Judges 7.7), that is, was their captain-general six years. So when Jotham upbraids the Shechemites with the obligation they had to Gideon, who had been their judge and ruler, he tells them, "He fought for you, and adventured[1] his life far, and delivered you out of the hands of Midian" (Judges 9.17). Nothing mentioned of him but what he did as a general: and indeed that is all is found in his history, or in any of the rest of the judges. And Abimelech particularly is called king, though at most he was but their general. And when, being weary of the ill conduct of Samuel's sons, the children of Israel desired a king, "like all the nations to judge them, and to go out before them, and to fight their battles" (1 Samuel 8.20), God granting their desire, says to Samuel, "I will send thee a man, and thou shalt anoint him to be captain over my people Israel, that he may save my people out of the hands of the Philistines" (9.16), as if the only business of a king had been to lead out their armies, and fight in their defense; and accordingly at his inauguration pouring a vial of oil upon him, declares to Saul, that "the Lord had anointed him to be captain over his inheritance" (10.1). And therefore those, who after Saul's being solemnly chosen and saluted king by the tribes at Mispah, were unwilling to have him their king, made no other objection but this, "How shall this man save us?" (5.27), as if they should have said, "This man is unfit to be our king, not having skill and conduct enough in war, to be able to defend us." And when God resolved to transfer the government to David, it is in these words, "But now thy kingdom shall not continue: the Lord has sought him a man after his own heart, and the Lord has commanded him to be captain over his people" (8.14), as if the whole kingly authority were nothing else but to be their general: and therefore the tribes who had stuck to Saul's family, and opposed David's reign, when they came to Hebron with terms of submission to him, they tell him, among other arguments they had to submit to him as to their king, that he was in effect their king

---

1   *adventured*   Risked.

in Saul's time, and therefore they had no reason but to receive him as their king now. "Also," say they, "in time past, when Saul was king over us, thou wast he that leddest out and broughtest in Israel, and the Lord said unto thee, 'Thou shalt feed my people Israel, and thou shalt be a captain over Israel.'"[1]

§ 110. Thus, whether a family by degrees grew up into a commonwealth, and the fatherly authority being continued on to the elder son, everyone in his turn growing up under it, tacitly submitted to it, and the easiness and equality of it not offending anyone, everyone acquiesced, till time seemed to have confirmed it, and settled a right of succession by prescription: or whether several families, or the descendants of several families, whom chance, neighborhood, or business brought together, uniting into society, the need of a general, whose conduct might defend them against their enemies in war, and the great confidence the innocence and sincerity of that poor but virtuous age, (such as are almost all those which begin governments, that ever come to last in the world) gave men one of another, made the first beginners of commonwealths generally put the rule into one man's hand, without any other express limitation or restraint, but what the nature of the thing, and the end of government required: which ever of those it was that at first put the rule into the hands of a single person, certain it is nobody was entrusted with it but for the public good and safety, and to those ends, in the infancies of commonwealths, those who had it commonly used it. And unless they had done so, young societies could not have subsisted; without such nursing fathers tender and careful of the public weal, all governments would have sunk under the weakness and infirmities of their infancy, and the prince and the people had soon perished together.

§ 111. But though the golden age (before vain ambition, and amor sceleratus habendi,[2] evil concupiscence,[3] had corrupted men's minds into a mistake of true power and honor) had more virtue, and consequently better governors, as well as less vicious subjects, and there was then no stretching prerogative on the one side, to oppress the people; nor consequently on the other, any dispute about privilege, to lessen or restrain the power of the magistrate, and so no contest betwixt rulers and people about governors or government:[4] yet, when ambi-

---

1   2 Samuel 5.2.

2   *amor sceleratus habendi*   Latin: accursed love of possessing.

3   *concupiscence*   Lust.

4   *nor consequently ... governors or government*   [Locke's note] "At first, when some certain kind of regiment was once approved, it may be nothing was then farther thought upon for the manner of governing, but all permitted unto their wisdom and discretion which were to rule, till by experience they *(continued)*

tion and luxury in future ages would retain and increase the power, without doing the business for which it was given; and aided by flattery, taught princes to have distinct and separate interests from their people, men found it necessary to examine more carefully the original and rights of government; and to find out ways to restrain the exorbitances, and prevent the abuses of that power, which they having entrusted in another's hands only for their own good, they found was made use of to hurt them.

§ 112. Thus we may see how probable it is, that people that were naturally free, and by their own consent either submitted to the government of their father, or united together out of different families to make a government, should generally put the rule into one man's hands, and choose to be under the conduct of a single person, without so much as by express conditions limiting or regulating his power, which they thought safe enough in his honesty and prudence; though they never dreamed of monarchy being jure Divino,[1] which we never heard of among mankind, till it was revealed to us by the divinity of this last age; nor ever allowed paternal power to have a right to dominion, or to be the foundation of all government. And thus much may suffice to show, that as far as we have any light from history, we have reason to conclude, that all peaceful beginnings of government have been laid in the consent of the people. I say peaceful, because I shall have occasion in another place to speak of conquest, which some esteem a way of beginning of governments.

The other objection I find urged against the beginning of polities, in the way I have mentioned, is this, viz.

§ 113. That all men being born under government, some or other,[2] it is impossible any of them should ever be free, and at liberty to unite together, and begin a new one, or ever be able to erect a lawful government.

If this argument be good; I ask, how came so many lawful monarchies into the world? for if anybody, upon this supposition, can show me any one man in any age of the world free to begin a lawful monarchy, I will be bound to show him ten other free men at liberty, at the same time to unite and begin a new government under a regal, or any

---

found this for all parts very inconvenient, so as the thing which they had devised for a remedy, did indeed but increase the sore which it should have cured. They saw, that to live by one man's will, became the cause of all men's misery. This constrained them to come unto laws wherein all men might see their duty before hand, and know the penalties of transgressing them" (Hooker, *Ecclesiastical Polity Lib.* 1. sect. 10).

1   *jure Divino*   Latin: by divine right.

2   *government, some or other*   Some government or other.

other form; it being demonstration, that if anyone, born under the dominion of another, may be so free as to have a right to command others in a new and distinct empire, everyone that is born under the dominion of another may be so free too, and may become a ruler, or subject, of a distinct separate government. And so by this their own principle, either all men, however born, are free, or else there is but one lawful prince, one lawful government in the world. And then they have nothing to do, but barely to show us which that is; which when they have done, I doubt not but all mankind will easily agree to pay obedience to him.

§ 114. Though it be a sufficient answer to their objection, to show that it involves them in the same difficulties that it does those they use it against; yet I shall endeavor to discover the weakness of this argument a little farther. "All men," say they, "are born under government, and therefore they cannot be at liberty to begin a new one. Everyone is born a subject to his father, or his prince, and is therefore under the perpetual tie of subjection and allegiance." It is plain mankind never owned nor considered any such natural subjection that they were born in, to one or to the other that tied them, without their own consents, to a subjection to them and their heirs.

§ 115. For there are no examples so frequent in history, both sacred and profane,[1] as those of men withdrawing themselves, and their obedience, from the jurisdiction they were born under, and the family or community they were bred up in, and setting up new governments in other places; from whence sprang all that number of petty commonwealths in the beginning of ages, and which always multiplied, as long as there was room enough, till the stronger, or more fortunate, swallowed the weaker; and those great ones again breaking to pieces, dissolved into lesser dominions. All [of] which are so many testimonies against paternal sovereignty, and plainly prove, that it was not the natural right of the father descending to his heirs, that made governments in the beginning, since it was impossible, upon that ground, there should have been so many little kingdoms; all must have been but only one universal monarchy, if men had not been at liberty to separate themselves from their families, and the government, be it what it will, that was set up in it, and go and make distinct commonwealths and other governments, as they thought fit.

§ 116. This has been the practice of the world from its first beginning to this day; nor is it now any more hindrance to the freedom of mankind, that they are born under constituted and ancient polities, that have established laws, and set forms of government, than if they were

---

1 *profane* Secular—not involved with religion.

born in the woods, among the unconfined inhabitants, that run loose in them: for those, who would persuade us, that by being born under any government, we are naturally subjects to it, and have no more any title or pretence to the freedom of the state of nature, have no other reason (bating[1] that of paternal power, which we have already answered) to produce for it, but only, because our fathers or progenitors[2] passed away their natural liberty, and thereby bound up themselves and their posterity to a perpetual subjection to the government, which they themselves submitted to. It is true, that whatever engagements or promises anyone has made for himself, he is under the obligation of them, but cannot, by any compact whatsoever, bind his children or posterity: for his son, when a man, being altogether as free as the father, any act of the father can no more give away the liberty of the son, than it can of anybody else: he may indeed annex such conditions to the land, he enjoyed as a subject of any commonwealth, as may oblige his son to be of that community, if he will enjoy those possessions which were his father's; because that estate being his father's property, he may dispose, or settle it, as he pleases.

§ 117. And this has generally given the occasion to mistake in this matter; because commonwealths not permitting any part of their dominions to be dismembered, nor to be enjoyed by any but those of their community, the son cannot ordinarily enjoy the possessions of his father, but under the same terms his father did, by becoming a member of the society; whereby he puts himself presently under the government he finds there established, as much as any other subject of that commonwealth. And thus the consent of freemen, born under government, which only makes them members of it, being given separately in their turns, as each comes to be of age, and not in a multitude together; people take no notice of it, and thinking it not done at all, or not necessary, conclude they are naturally subjects as they are men.

§ 118. But, it is plain, governments themselves understand it otherwise; they claim no power over the son, because of that they had over the father; nor look on children as being their subjects, by their fathers being so. If a subject of England have a child, by an English woman in France, whose subject is he? Not the king of England's; for he must have leave to be admitted to the privileges of it: nor the king of France's; for how then has his father a liberty to bring him away, and breed him as he pleases? and who ever was judged as a traitor or deserter, if he left, or warred against a country, for being barely born in it of parents that were aliens there? It is plain then, by the practice of

---

1 *bating*   Excepting.
2 *progenitors*   Ancestors.

governments themselves, as well as by the law of right reason, that a child is born a subject of no country or government. He is under his father's tuition and authority, till he comes to age of discretion; and then he is a freeman, at liberty what government he will put himself under, what body politic he will unite himself to: for if an Englishman's son, born in France, be at liberty, and may do so, it is evident there is no tie upon him by his father's being a subject of this kingdom; nor is he bound up by any compact of his ancestors. And why then has not his son, by the same reason, the same liberty, though he be born anywhere else? Since the power that a father has naturally over his children, is the same, where-ever they be born, and the ties of natural obligations, are not bounded by the positive limits of kingdoms and commonwealths.

§ 119. Every man being, as has been shown, naturally free, and nothing being able to put him into subjection to any earthly power, but only his own consent; it is to be considered, what shall be understood to be a sufficient declaration of a man's consent, to make him subject to the laws of any government. There is a common distinction of an express and a tacit consent, which will concern our present case. Nobody doubts but an express consent, of any man entering into any society, makes him a perfect member of that society, a subject of that government. The difficulty is, what ought to be looked upon as a tacit consent, and how far it binds, i.e., how far anyone shall be looked on to have consented, and thereby submitted to any government, where he has made no expressions of it at all. And to this I say, that every man, that has any possessions, or enjoyment, of any part of the dominions of any government, does thereby give his tacit consent, and is as far forth obliged to obedience to the laws of that government, during such enjoyment, as anyone under it; whether this his possession be of land, to him and his heirs forever, or a lodging only for a week; or whether it be barely traveling freely on the highway; and in effect, it reaches as far as the very being of anyone within the territories of that government.

§ 120. To understand this the better, it is fit to consider, that every man, when he at first incorporates himself into any commonwealth, he, by his uniting himself thereunto, annexed also, and submits to the community, those possessions, which he has, or shall acquire, that do not already belong to any other government: for it would be a direct contradiction, for anyone to enter into society with others for the securing and regulating of property; and yet to suppose his land, whose property is to be regulated by the laws of the society, should be exempt from the jurisdiction of that government, to which he himself, the proprietor of the land, is a subject. By the same act therefore, whereby

anyone unites his person, which was before free, to any commonwealth, by the same he unites his possessions, which were before free,
to it also; and they become, both of them, person and possession, subject to the government and dominion of that commonwealth, as long
as it has a being. Whoever therefore, from thenceforth, by inheritance,
purchase, permission, or otherwise, enjoys any part of the land, so annexed to, and under the government of that commonwealth, must take
it with the condition it is under; that is, of submitting to the government
of the commonwealth, under whose jurisdiction it is, as far forth as
any subject of it.

§ 121. But since the government has a direct jurisdiction only over
the land, and reaches the possessor of it, (before he has actually incorporated himself in the society) only as he dwells upon, and enjoys
that; the obligation anyone is under, by virtue of such enjoyment, to
submit to the government, begins and ends with the enjoyment; so that
whenever the owner, who has given nothing but such a tacit consent
to the government, will, by donation, sale, or otherwise, quit the said
possession, he is at liberty to go and incorporate himself into any other
commonwealth; or to agree with others to begin a new one, in vacuis
locis,[1] in any part of the world, they can find free and unpossessed:
whereas he, that has once, by actual agreement, and any express declaration, given his consent to be of any commonwealth, is perpetually
and indispensably obliged to be, and remain unalterably a subject to it,
and can never be again in the liberty of the state of nature; unless, by
any calamity, the government he was under comes to be dissolved; or
else by some public act cuts him off from being any longer a member
of it.

§ 122. But submitting to the laws of any country, living quietly, and
enjoying privileges and protection under them, makes not a man a
member of that society: this is only a local protection and homage due
to and from all those, who, not being in a state of war, come within the
territories belonging to any government, to all parts whereof the force
of its laws extends. But this no more makes a man a member of that
society, a perpetual subject of that commonwealth, than it would make
a man a subject to another, in whose family he found it convenient to
abide for some time; though, while he continued in it, he were obliged
to comply with the laws, and submit to the government he found there.
And thus we see, that foreigners, by living all their lives under another
government, and enjoying the privileges and protection of it, though
they are bound, even in conscience, to submit to its administration, as
far forth as any denizen; yet do not thereby come to be subjects or

---

1   *in vacuis locis*   Latin: in empty places.

members of that commonwealth. Nothing can make any man so, but his actually entering into it by positive engagement, and express promise and compact. This is that, which I think, concerning the beginning of political societies, and that consent which makes anyone a member of any commonwealth.

Chapter 9. Of the Ends[1] of Political Society and Government

§ 123. If man in the state of nature be so free, as has been said; if he be absolute lord of his own person and possessions, equal to the greatest, and subject to nobody, why will he part with his freedom? why will he give up this empire, and subject himself to the dominion and control of any other power? To which it is obvious to answer, that though in the state of nature he has such a right, yet the enjoyment of it is very uncertain, and constantly exposed to the invasion of others: for all being kings as much as he, every man his equal, and the greater part no strict observers of equity and justice, the enjoyment of the property he has in this state is very unsafe, very insecure. This makes him willing to quit a condition, which, however free, is full of fears and continual dangers: and it is not without reason, that he seeks out, and is willing to join in society with others, who are already united, or have a mind to unite, for the mutual preservation of their lives, liberties and estates, which I call by the general name, property.

§ 124. The great and chief end, therefore, of men's uniting into commonwealths, and putting themselves under government, is the preservation of their property. To which in the state of nature there are many things wanting.

First, There wants an established, settled, known law, received and allowed by common consent to be the standard of right and wrong, and the common measure to decide all controversies between them: for though the law of nature be plain and intelligible to all rational creatures; yet men being biased by their interest, as well as ignorant for want of study of it, are not apt to allow of it as a law binding to them in the application of it to their particular cases.

§ 125. Secondly, In the state of nature there wants a known and indifferent judge, with authority to determine all differences according to the established law: for everyone in that state being both judge and executioner of the law of nature, men being partial to themselves, passion and revenge is very apt to carry them too far, and with too much heat, in their own cases; as well as negligence, and unconcernedness, to make them too remiss in other men's.

---

1 *Ends* Purposes.

§ 126. Thirdly, In the state of nature there often wants power to back and support the sentence when right, and to give it due execution. They who by any injustice offended, will seldom fail, where they are able, by force to make good their injustice; such resistance many times makes the punishment dangerous, and frequently destructive, to those who attempt it.

§ 127. Thus mankind, notwithstanding all the privileges of the state of nature, being but in an ill condition, while they remain in it, are quickly driven into society. Hence it comes to pass, that we seldom find any number of men live any time together in this state. The inconveniencies that they are therein exposed to, by the irregular and uncertain exercise of the power every man has of punishing the transgressions of others, make them take sanctuary under the established laws of government, and therein seek the preservation of their property. It is this makes them so willingly give up everyone his single power of punishing, to be exercised by such alone, as shall be appointed to it among them; and by such rules as the community, or those authorized by them to that purpose, shall agree on. And in this we have the original right and rise of both the legislative and executive power, as well as of the governments and societies themselves.

§ 128. For in the state of nature, to omit the liberty he has of innocent[1] delights, a man has two powers.

The first is to do whatsoever he thinks fit for the preservation of himself, and others within the permission of the law of nature: by which law, common to them all, he and all the rest of mankind are one community, make up one society, distinct from all other creatures. And were it not for the corruption and viciousness of degenerate men, there would be no need of any other; no necessity that men should separate from this great and natural community, and by positive agreements combine into smaller and divided associations.

The other power a man has in the state of nature, is the power to punish the crimes committed against that law. Both these he gives up, when he joins in a private, if I may so call it, or particular politic society, and incorporates into any commonwealth, separate from the rest of mankind.

§ 129. The first power, viz. of doing whatsoever he thought for the preservation of himself, and the rest of mankind, he gives up to be regulated by laws made by the society, so far forth as the preservation of himself, and the rest of that society shall require; which laws of the society in many things confine the liberty he had by the law of nature.

---

1   *innocent*   Harmless in intention.

§ 130. Secondly, The power of punishing he wholly gives up, and engages his natural force, (which he might before employ in the execution of the law of nature, by his own single authority, as he thought fit) to assist the executive power of the society, as the law thereof shall require: for being now in a new state, wherein he is to enjoy many conveniences, from the labor, assistance, and society of others in the same community, as well as protection from its whole strength; he is to part also with as much of his natural liberty, in providing for himself, as the good, prosperity, and safety of the society shall require; which is not only necessary, but just, since the other members of the society do the like.

§ 131. But though men, when they enter into society, give up the equality, liberty, and executive power they had in the state of nature, into the hands of the society, to be so far disposed of by the legislative, as the good of the society shall require; yet it being only with an intention in everyone the better to preserve himself, his liberty and property; (for no rational creature can be supposed to change his condition with an intention to be worse) the power of the society, or legislative constituted by them, can never be supposed to extend farther, than the common good; but is obliged to secure everyone's property, by providing against those three defects above mentioned, that made the state of nature so unsafe and uneasy. And so whoever has the legislative or supreme power of any commonwealth, is bound to govern by established standing laws, promulgated and known to the people, and not by extemporary[1] decrees; by indifferent and upright judges, who are to decide controversies by those laws; and to employ the force of the community at home, only in the execution of such laws, or abroad to prevent or redress foreign injuries, and secure the community from inroads and invasion. And all this to be directed to no other end, but the peace, safety, and public good of the people.

Chapter 10. Of the Forms of a Commonwealth

§ 132. The majority having, as has been shown, upon men's first uniting into society, the whole power of the community naturally in them, may employ all that power in making laws for the community from time to time, and executing those laws by officers of their own appointing; and then the form of the government is a perfect democracy: or else may put the power of making laws into the hands of a few select men, and their heirs or successors; and then it is an oligarchy: or else into the hands of one man, and then it is a monarchy: if to him and

---

1 *extemporary* Makeshift, without preparation.

his heirs, it is an hereditary monarchy: if to him only for life, but upon his death the power only of nominating a successor to return to them; an elective monarchy. And so accordingly of these the community may make compounded and mixed forms of government, as they think good. And if the legislative power be at first given by the majority to one or more persons only for their lives, or any limited time, and then the supreme power to revert to them again; when it is so reverted, the community may dispose of it again anew into what hands they please, and so constitute a new form of government: for the form of government depending upon the placing the supreme power, which is the legislative, it being impossible to conceive that an inferior power should prescribe to a superior, or any but the supreme make laws, according as the power of making laws is placed, such is the form of the commonwealth.

§ 133. By "commonwealth," I must be understood all along to mean, not a democracy, or any form of government, but any independent community, which the Latins signified by the word *civitas*, to which the word which best answers in our language, is "commonwealth," and most properly expresses such a society of men, which "community" or "city" in English does not; for there may be subordinate communities in a government; and city among us has a quite different notion from commonwealth: and therefore, to avoid ambiguity, I crave leave to use the word commonwealth in that sense, in which I find it used by King James the First;[1] and I take it to be its genuine signification; which if anybody dislike, I consent with him to change it for a better.

Chapter 11. Of the Extent of the Legislative Power

§ 134. The great end of men's entering into society, being the enjoyment of their properties in peace and safety, and the great instrument and means of that being the laws established in that society; the first and fundamental positive law of all commonwealths is the establishing of the legislative power; as the first and fundamental natural law, which is to govern even the legislative itself, is the preservation of the society, and (as far as will consist with the public good) of every person in it. This legislative is not only the supreme power of the commonwealth, but sacred and unalterable in the hands where the community have once placed it; nor can any edict of anybody else, in whatever form conceived, or by whatever power backed, have the

---

1   *King James the First*   James I (1566-1625) ruled England from 1603 to 1625. His writings strongly supported the theory of the divine right of kings.

force and obligation of a law, which has not its sanction from that legislative[1] which the public has chosen and appointed: for without this the law could not have that, which is absolutely necessary to its being a law,[2] the consent of the society, over whom nobody can have a power to make laws, but by their own consent, and by authority received from them; and therefore all the obedience, which by the most solemn ties anyone can be obliged to pay, ultimately terminates in this supreme power, and is directed by those laws which it enacts: nor can any oaths to any foreign power whatsoever, or any domestic subordinate power, discharge any member of the society from his obedience to the legislative, acting pursuant to their trust; nor oblige him to any obedience contrary to the laws so enacted, or farther than they do allow; it being ridiculous to imagine one can be tied ultimately to obey any power in the society, which is not the supreme.

§ 135. Though the legislative, whether placed in one or more, whether it be always in being, or only by intervals, though it be the supreme power in every commonwealth; yet,

First, It is not, nor can possibly be absolutely arbitrary over the lives and fortunes of the people: for it being but the joint power of every member of the society given up to that person, or assembly, which is legislator; it can be no more than those persons had in a state of nature before they entered into society, and gave up to the community: for nobody can transfer to another more power than he has in himself; and nobody has an absolute arbitrary power over himself, or over any other, to destroy his own life, or take away the life or property of another. A man, as has been proved, cannot subject himself to the arbitrary power of another; and having in the state of nature no arbitrary power over the life, liberty, or possession of another, but only so much

---

1 *legislative* Legislator.

2 *for without this the law ... necessary to its being a law* [Locke's note] "The lawful power of making laws to command whole politic societies of men, belonging so properly unto the same entire societies, that for any prince or potentate of whatever kind upon earth, to exercise the same of himself, and not by express commission immediately and personally received from God, or else by authority derived at the first from their consent, upon whose persons they impose laws, it is no better than mere tyranny. Laws they are not therefore which public approbation has not made so" (Hooker, *Ecclesiastical Polity Lib.* I. sect. 10). "Of this point therefore we are to note, that men naturally have no full and perfect power to command whole politic multitudes of men, therefore utterly without our consent, we could in such sort be at no man's commandment living. And to be commanded we do consent, when that society, whereof we be a part, hath at any time before consented, without revoking the same after by the like universal agreement. Laws therefore human, of what kind so ever, are available by consent" (*Ibid.*).

as the law of nature gave him for the preservation of himself, and the rest of mankind; this is all he does, or can give up to the commonwealth, and by it to the legislative power, so that the legislative can have no more than this. Their power, in the utmost bounds of it, is limited to the public good of the society.[1] It is a power, that has no other end but preservation, and therefore can never have a right to destroy, enslave, or designedly to impoverish the subjects. The obligations of the law of nature cease not in society, but only in many cases are drawn closer, and have by human laws known penalties annexed to them, to enforce their observation. Thus the law of nature stands as an eternal rule to all men, legislators as well as others. The rules that they make for other men's actions, must, as well as their own and other men's actions, be conformable to the law of nature, i.e., to the will of God, of which that is a declaration, and the fundamental law of nature being the preservation of mankind, no human sanction can be good, or valid against it.

§ 136. Secondly, The legislative, or supreme authority, cannot assume to its self a power to rule by extemporary arbitrary decrees, but is bound to dispense justice, and decide the rights of the subject by promulgated standing laws,[2] and known authorized judges: for the law of nature being unwritten, and so no where to be found but in the minds of men, they who through passion or interest shall miscite,[3] or

---

1   *Their power ... public good of the society*   [Locke's note] "Two foundations there are which bear up public societies; the one a natural inclination, whereby all men desire sociable life and fellowship; the other an order, expressly or secretly agreed upon, touching the manner of their union in living together: the latter is that which we call the law of a commonweal, the very soul of a politic body, the parts whereof are by law animated, held together, and set on work in such actions as the common good requires. Laws politic, ordained for external order and regiment among men, are never framed as they should be, unless presuming the will of man to be inwardly obstinate, rebellious, and averse from all obedience to the sacred laws of his nature; in a word, unless presuming man to be, in regard of his depraved mind, little better than a wild beast, they do accordingly provide, notwithstanding, so to frame his outward actions, that they be no hindrance unto the common good, for which societies are instituted. Unless they do this, they are not perfect" (Hooker, *Ecclesiastical Polity Lib.* i. sect. 10).
2   *The legislative ... promulgated standing laws*   [Locke's note] "Human laws are measures in respect of men whose actions they must direct, howbeit such measures they are as have also their higher rules to be measured by, which rules are two, the law of God, and the law of nature; so that laws human must be made according to the general laws of nature, and without contradiction to any positive law of scripture, otherwise they are ill made" (Hooker, *Ecclesiastical Polity Lib.* 3. sect. 9). "To constrain men to any thing inconvenient does seem unreasonable" (Ibid. i. sect. 10).
3   *miscite*   Cite erroneously.

misapply it, cannot so easily be convinced of their mistake where there is no established judge: and so it serves not, as it ought, to determine the rights, and fence the properties of those that live under it, especially where everyone is judge, interpreter, and executioner of it too, and that in his own case: and he that has right on his side, having ordinarily but his own single strength, has not force enough to defend himself from injuries, or to punish delinquents. To avoid these inconveniencies, which disorder men's properties in the state of nature, men unite into societies, that they may have the united strength of the whole society to secure and defend their properties, and may have standing rules to bound it, by which everyone may know what is his. To this end it is that men give up all their natural power to the society which they enter into, and the community put the legislative power into such hands as they think fit, with this trust, that they shall be governed by declared laws, or else their peace, quiet, and property will still be at the same uncertainty, as it was in the state of nature.

§ 137. Absolute arbitrary power, or governing without settled standing laws, can neither of them consist with[1] the ends of society and government, which men would not quit the freedom of the state of nature for, and tie themselves up under, were it not to preserve their lives, liberties and fortunes, and by stated rules of right and property to secure their peace and quiet. It cannot be supposed that they should intend, had they a power so to do, to give to anyone, or more, an absolute arbitrary power over their persons and estates, and put a force into the magistrate's hand to execute his unlimited will arbitrarily upon them. This were to put themselves into a worse condition than the state of nature, wherein they had a liberty to defend their right against the injuries of others, and were upon equal terms of force to maintain it, whether invaded by a single man, or many in combination. Whereas by supposing they have given up themselves to the absolute arbitrary power and will of a legislator, they have disarmed themselves, and armed him, to make a prey of them when he pleases; he being in a much worse condition, who is exposed to the arbitrary power of one man, who has the command of 100,000, than he that is exposed to the arbitrary power of 100,000 single men; nobody being secure, that his will, who has such a command, is better than that of other men, though his force be 100,000 times stronger. And therefore, whatever form the commonwealth is under, the ruling power ought to govern by declared and received laws, and not by extemporary dictates and undetermined[2] resolutions: for then mankind will be in a far worse condition than in

---

1   *can neither of them consist with*   Cannot be consistent with.
2   *undetermined*   Not settled or fixed.

the state of nature, if they shall have armed one, or a few men with the joint power of a multitude, to force them to obey at pleasure the exorbitant and unlimited decrees of their sudden thoughts, or unrestrained, and till that moment unknown wills, without having any measures set down which may guide and justify their actions: for all the power the government has, being only for the good of the society, as it ought not to be arbitrary and at pleasure, so it ought to be exercised by established and promulgated laws; that both the people may know their duty, and be safe and secure within the limits of the law; and the rulers too kept within their bounds, and not be tempted, by the power they have in their hands, to employ it to such purposes, and by such measures, as they would not have known, and own not willingly.

§ 138. Thirdly, The supreme power cannot take from any man any part of his property without his own consent: for the preservation of property being the end of government, and that for which men enter into society, it necessarily supposes and requires, that the people should have property, without which they must be supposed to lose that, by entering into society, which was the end for which they entered into it; too gross an absurdity for any man to own.[1] Men therefore in society having property, they have such a right to the goods, which by the law of the community are theirs, that nobody has a right to take their substance or any part of it from them, without their own consent: without this they have no property at all; for I have truly no property in that, which another can by right take from me, when he pleases, against my consent. Hence it is a mistake to think, that the supreme or legislative power of any commonwealth, can do what it will, and dispose of the estates of the subject arbitrarily, or take any part of them at pleasure. This is not much to be feared in governments where the legislative consists, wholly or in part, in assemblies which are variable, whose members, upon the dissolution of the assembly, are subjects under the common laws of their country, equally with the rest. But in governments, where the legislative is in one lasting assembly always in being, or in one man, as in absolute monarchies, there is danger still, that they will think themselves to have a distinct interest from the rest of the community; and so will be apt to increase their own riches and power, by taking what they think fit from the people: for a man's property is not at all secure, though there be good and equitable laws to set the bounds of it between him and his fellow subjects, if he who commands those subjects have power to take from any private man, what part he pleases of his property, and use and dispose of it as he thinks good.

---

1 *own* Accept.

§ 139. But government, into whatsoever hands it is put, being, as I have before shown, entrusted with this condition, and for this end, that men might have and secure their properties; the prince, or senate, however it may have power to make laws, for the regulating of property between the subjects one among another, yet can never have a power to take to themselves the whole, or any part of the subjects property, without their own consent: for this would be in effect to leave them no property at all. And to let us see, that even absolute power, where it is necessary, is not arbitrary by being absolute, but is still limited by that reason, and confined to those ends, which required it in some cases to be absolute, we need look no farther than the common practice of martial[1] discipline: for the preservation of the army, and in it of the whole commonwealth, requires an absolute obedience to the command of every superior officer, and it is justly death to disobey or dispute the most dangerous or unreasonable of them; but yet we see, that neither the sergeant, that could command a soldier to march up to the mouth of a cannon, or stand in a breach,[2] where he is almost sure to perish, can command that soldier to give him one penny of his money; nor the general, that can condemn him to death for deserting his post, or for not obeying the most desperate orders, can yet, with all his absolute power of life and death, dispose of one farthing[3] of that soldier's estate, or seize one jot[4] of his goods; whom yet he can command any thing, and hang for the least disobedience; because such a blind obedience is necessary to that end, for which the commander has his power, viz. the preservation of the rest; but the disposing of his goods has nothing to do with it.

§ 140. It is true, governments cannot be supported without great charge,[5] and it is fit everyone who enjoys his share of the protection, should pay out of his estate his proportion for the maintenance of it. But still it must be with his own consent, i.e., the consent of the majority, giving it either by themselves, or their representatives chosen by them: for if anyone shall claim a power to lay and levy taxes on the people, by his own authority, and without such consent of the people, he thereby invades the fundamental law of property, and subverts the end of government: for what property have I in that, which another may by right take, when he pleases, to himself?

---

1 *martial* Concerning soldiers.
2 *breach* Gap in a fortification.
3 *farthing* Smallest-valued British coin, worth a quarter of a penny—almost nothing.
4 *jot* Tiny bit.
5 *charge* Expense.

§ 141. Fourthly, The legislative cannot transfer the power of making laws to any other hands: for it being but a delegated power from the people, they who have it cannot pass it over to others. The people alone can appoint the form of the commonwealth, which is by constituting the legislative, and appointing in whose hands that shall be. And when the people have said, We will submit to rules, and be governed by laws made by such men, and in such forms, nobody else can say other men shall make laws for them; nor can the people be bound by any laws, but such as are enacted by those whom they have chosen, and authorized to make laws for them. The power of the legislative, being derived from the people by a positive voluntary grant and institution, can be no other than what that positive grant conveyed, which being only to make laws, and not to make legislators, the legislative can have no power to transfer their authority of making laws, and place it in other hands.

§ 142. These are the bounds which the trust, that is put in them by the society, and the law of God and nature, have set to the legislative power of every commonwealth, in all forms of government.

First, They are to govern by promulgated established laws, not to be varied in particular cases, but to have one rule for rich and poor, for the favorite at court, and the country man at plow.

Secondly, These laws also ought to be designed for no other end ultimately, but the good of the people.

Thirdly, They must not raise taxes on the property of the people, without the consent of the people, given by themselves, or their deputies. And this properly concerns only such governments where the legislative is always in being, or at least where the people have not reserved any part of the legislative to deputies, to be from time to time chosen by themselves.

Fourthly, The legislative neither must nor can transfer the power of making laws to anybody else, or place it anywhere, but where the people have placed it.

Chapter 12. Of the Legislative, Executive, and Federative Power of the Commonwealth

§ 143. The legislative power is that, which has a right to direct how the force of the commonwealth shall be employed for preserving the community and the members of it. But because those laws which are constantly to be executed, and whose force is always to continue, may be made in a little time; therefore there is no need, that the legislative should be always in being, not having always business to do. And because it may be too great a temptation to human frailty, apt to grasp at power, for the same persons, who have the power of making laws, to have also in their hands the power to execute them, whereby they may exempt themselves from obedience to the laws they make, and suit the law, both in its making, and execution, to their own private advantage, and thereby come to have a distinct interest from the rest of the community, contrary to the end of society and government: therefore in well ordered commonwealths, where the good of the whole is so considered, as it ought, the legislative power is put into the hands of divers[1] persons, who duly assembled, have by themselves, or jointly with others, a power to make laws, which when they have done, being separated again, they are themselves subject to the laws they have made; which is a new and near tie upon them, to take care, that they make them for the public good.

§ 144. But because the laws, that are at once, and in a short time made, have a constant and lasting force, and need a perpetual execution, or an attendance thereunto; therefore it is necessary there should be a power always in being, which should see to the execution of the laws that are made, and remain in force. And thus the legislative and executive power come often to be separated.

§ 145. There is another power in every commonwealth, which one may call natural, because it is that which answers to the power every man naturally had before he entered into society: for though in a commonwealth the members of it are distinct persons still in reference to one another, and as such are governed by the laws of the society; yet in reference to the rest of mankind, they make one body, which is, as every member of it before was, still in the state of nature with the rest of mankind. Hence it is, that the controversies that happen between any man of the society with those that are out of it, are managed by the public; and an injury done to a member of their body, engages the whole in the reparation of it. So that under this consideration, the whole community is one body in the state of nature, in respect of all other states or persons out of its community.

§ 146. This therefore contains the power of war and peace, leagues and alliances, and all the transactions, with all persons and communities without the commonwealth, and may be called federative, if anyone pleases. So[2] the thing be understood, I am indifferent as to the name.

§ 147. These two powers, executive and federative, though they be really distinct in themselves, yet one comprehending the execution of the municipal laws of the society within itself, upon all that are parts

---

1 *divers* Several.
2 *So* As long as.

of it; the other the management of the security and interest of the public without, with all those that it may receive benefit or damage from, yet they are always almost united. And though this federative power in the well or ill management of it be of great moment[1] to the commonwealth, yet it is much less capable to be directed by antecedent, standing, positive laws, than the executive; and so must necessarily be left to the prudence and wisdom of those, whose hands it is in, to be managed for the public good: for the laws that concern subjects one among another, being to direct their actions, may well enough precede them. But what is to be done in reference to foreigners, depending much upon their actions, and the variation of designs and interests, must be left in great part to the prudence of those, who have this power committed to them, to be managed by the best of their skill, for the advantage of the commonwealth.

§ 148. Though, as I said, the executive and federative power of every community be really distinct in themselves, yet they are hardly to be separated, and placed at the same time, in the hands of distinct persons: for both of them requiring the force of the society for their exercise, it is almost impracticable[2] to place the force of the commonwealth in distinct, and not subordinate hands; or that the executive and federative power should be placed in persons, that might act separately, whereby the force of the public would be under different commands: which would be apt some time or other to cause disorder and ruin.

Chapter 13. Of the Subordination of the Powers of the Commonwealth

§ 149. Though in a constituted commonwealth, standing upon its own basis, and acting according to its own nature, that is, acting for the preservation of the community, there can be but one supreme power, which is the legislative, to which all the rest are and must be subordinate, yet the legislative being only a fiduciary power[3] to act for certain ends, there remains still in the people a supreme power to remove or alter the legislative, when they find the legislative act contrary to the trust reposed in them: for all power given with trust for the attaining an end, being limited by that end, whenever that end is manifestly neglected, or opposed, the trust must necessarily be forfeited, and the power devolve into the hands of those that gave it, who may place it

---

1 *moment* Importance.

2 *impracticable* Impossible.

3 *fiduciary power* The power of a trustee—that is, the power to act on behalf of others.

anew where they shall think best for their safety and security. And thus the community perpetually retains a supreme power of saving themselves from the attempts[1] and designs of anybody, even of their legislators, whenever they shall be so foolish, or so wicked, as to lay and carry on designs against the liberties and properties of the subject: for no man or society of men, having a power to deliver up their preservation, or consequently the means of it, to the absolute will and arbitrary dominion of another; whenever anyone shall go about to bring them into such a slavish condition, they will always have a right to preserve, what they have not a power to part with; and to rid themselves of those, who invade this fundamental, sacred, and unalterable law of self-preservation, for which they entered into society. And thus the community may be said in this respect to be always the supreme power, but not as considered under any form of government, because this power of the people can never take place till the government be dissolved.

§ 150. In all cases, while the government subsists, the legislative is the supreme power: for what can give laws to another, must needs be superior to him; and since the legislative is no otherwise legislative of the society, but[2] by the right it has to make laws for all the parts, and for every member of the society, prescribing rules to their actions, and giving power of execution, where they are transgressed, the legislative must needs be the supreme, and all other powers, in any members or parts of the society, derived from and subordinate to it.

§ 151. In some commonwealths, where the legislative is not always in being, and the executive is vested in a single person, who has also a share in the legislative; there that single person in a very tolerable sense may also be called supreme: not that he has in himself all the supreme power, which is that of lawmaking; but because he has in him the supreme execution, from whom all inferior magistrates derive all their several subordinate powers, or at least the greatest part of them: having also no legislative superior to him, there being no law to be made without his consent, which cannot be expected should ever subject him to the other part of the legislative, he is properly enough in this sense supreme. But yet it is to be observed, that though oaths of allegiance and fealty are taken to him, it is not to him as supreme legislator, but as supreme executor of the law, made by a joint power of him with others; allegiance being nothing but an obedience according to law, which when he violates, he has no right to obedience, nor can claim it otherwise than as the public person vested with the power of

---

1   *attempts*   Attacks.
2   *no otherwise ... but*   In no other way ... except.

the law, and so is to be considered as the image, phantom, or representative of the commonwealth, acted by the will of the society, declared in its laws; and thus he has no will, no power, but that of the law. But when he quits this representation, this public will, and acts by his own private will, he degrades himself, and is but a single private person without power, and without will, that has any right to obedience; the members owing no obedience but to the public will of the society.

§ 152. The executive power, placed anywhere but in a person that has also a share in the legislative, is visibly subordinate and accountable to it, and may be at pleasure changed and displaced; so that it is not the supreme executive power, that is exempt from subordination, but the supreme executive power vested in one, who having a share in the legislative, has no distinct superior legislative to be subordinate and accountable to, farther than he himself shall join and consent; so that he is no more subordinate than he himself shall think fit, which one may certainly conclude will be but very little. Of other ministerial and subordinate powers in a commonwealth, we need not speak, they being so multiplied with infinite variety, in the different customs and constitutions of distinct commonwealths, that it is impossible to give a particular account of them all. Only thus much, which is necessary to our present purpose, we may take notice of concerning them, that they have no manner of authority, any of them, beyond what is by positive grant and commission delegated to them, and are all of them accountable to some other power in the commonwealth.

§ 153. It is not necessary, no, nor so much as convenient, that the legislative should be always in being; but absolutely necessary that the executive power should, because there is not always need of new laws to be made, but always need of execution of the laws that are made. When the legislative has put the execution of the laws, they make, into other hands, they have a power still to resume[1] it out of those hands, when they find cause, and to punish for any maladministration[2] against the laws. The same holds also in regard of the federative power, that and the executive being both ministerial and subordinate to the legislative, which, as has been shown, in a constituted commonwealth is the supreme. The legislative also in this case being supposed to consist of several persons, (for if it be a single person, it cannot but be always in being, and so will, as supreme, naturally have the supreme executive power, together with the legislative) may assemble, and exercise their legislature, at the times that either their original constitution, or their own adjournment, appoints, or when they

---

1   *resume*   Retake.
2   *maladministration*   Bad management.

please; if neither of these has appointed any time, or there be no other way prescribed to convoke[1] them: for the supreme power being placed in them by the people, it is always in them, and they may exercise it when they please, unless by their original constitution they are limited to certain seasons, or by an act of their supreme power they have adjourned to a certain time; and when that time comes, they have a right to assemble and act again.

§ 154. If the legislative, or any part of it, be made up of representatives chosen for that time by the people, which afterwards return into the ordinary state of subjects, and have no share in the legislature but upon a new choice, this power of choosing must also be exercised by the people, either at certain appointed seasons, or else when they are summoned to it; and in this latter case the power of convoking the legislative is ordinarily placed in the executive, and has one of these two limitations in respect of time: that either the original constitution requires their assembling and acting at certain intervals, and then the executive power does nothing but ministerially[2] issue directions for their electing and assembling, according to due forms; or else it is left to his prudence to call them by new elections, when the occasions or exigencies[3] of the public require the amendment of old, or making of new laws, or the redress or prevention of any inconveniencies, that lie on, or threaten the people.

§ 155. It may be demanded here, What if the executive power, being possessed of the force of the commonwealth, shall make use of that force to hinder the meeting and acting of the legislative, when the original constitution, or the public exigencies require it? I say, using force upon the people without authority, and contrary to the trust put in him that does so, is a state of war with the people, who have a right to reinstate their legislative in the exercise of their power: for having erected a legislative, with an intent they should exercise the power of making laws, either at certain set times, or when there is need of it, when they are hindered by any force from what is so necessary to the society, and wherein the safety and preservation of the people consists, the people have a right to remove it by force. In all states and conditions, the true remedy of force without authority, is to oppose force to it. The use of force without authority, always puts him that uses it into a state of war, as the aggressor, and renders him liable to be treated accordingly.

---

1 *convoke* Call together for a meeting.
2 *ministerially* In a capacity as minister; administratively.
3 *exigencies* Urgent needs.

§ 156. The power of assembling and dismissing the legislative, placed in the executive, gives not the executive a superiority over it, but is a fiduciary trust placed in him, for the safety of the people, in a case where the uncertainty and variableness of human affairs could not bear a steady fixed rule: for it not being possible, that the first framers of the government should, by any foresight, be so much masters of future events, as to be able to prefix so just periods of return and duration to the assemblies of the legislative, in all times to come, that might exactly answer all the exigencies of the commonwealth; the best remedy could be found for this defect, was to trust this to the prudence of one who was always to be present, and whose business it was to watch over the public good. Constant frequent meetings of the legislative, and long continuations of their assemblies, without necessary occasion, could not but be burdensome to the people, and must necessarily in time produce more dangerous inconveniencies, and yet the quick turn of affairs might be sometimes such as to need their present help: any delay of their convening might endanger the public; and sometimes too their business might be so great, that the limited time of their sitting might be too short for their work, and rob the public of that benefit which could be had only from their mature deliberation. What then could be done in this case to prevent the community from being exposed some time or other to eminent[1] hazard, on one side or the other, by fixed intervals and periods, set to the meeting and acting of the legislative, but to entrust it to the prudence of some, who being present, and acquainted with the state of public affairs, might make use of this prerogative for the public good? and where else could this be so well placed as in his hands, who was entrusted with the execution of the laws for the same end? Thus supposing the regulation of times for the assembling and sitting of the legislative, not settled by the original constitution, it naturally fell into the hands of the executive, not as an arbitrary power depending on his good pleasure, but with this trust always to have it exercised only for the public weal,[2] as the occurrences of times and change of affairs might require. Whether settled periods of their convening, or a liberty left to the prince for convoking the legislative, or perhaps a mixture of both, has the least inconvenience attending it, it is not my business here to inquire, but only to show, that though the executive power may have the prerogative of convoking and dissolving such conventions of the legislative, yet it is not thereby superior to it.

---

1   *eminent*   Noticeable.
2   *weal*   Well-being.

§ 157. Things of this world are in so constant a flux,[1] that nothing remains long in the same state. Thus people, riches, trade, power, change their stations, flourishing mighty cities come to ruin, and prove in times neglected desolate corners, while other unfrequented places grow into populous countries, filled with wealth and inhabitants. But things not always changing equally, and private interest often keeping up customs and privileges, when the reasons of them are ceased, it often comes to pass, that in governments, where part of the legislative consists of representatives chosen by the people, that in tract of time this representation becomes very unequal and disproportionate to the reasons it was at first established upon. To what gross absurdities the following of custom, when reason has left it, may lead, we may be satisfied, when we see the bare name of a town, of which there remains not so much as the ruins, where scarce so much housing as a sheepcote[2] or more inhabitants than a shepherd is to be found, sends as many representatives to the grand assembly of law-makers, as a whole county numerous in people, and powerful in riches. This strangers stand amazed at, and everyone must confess needs a remedy; though most think it hard to find one, because the constitution of the legislative being the original and supreme act of the society, antecedent to all positive laws in it, and depending wholly on the people, no inferior power can alter it. And therefore the people, when the legislative is once constituted, having, in such a government as we have been speaking of, no power to act as long as the government stands; this inconvenience is thought incapable of a remedy.

§ 158. Salus populi suprema lex,[3] is certainly so just and fundamental a rule, that he, who sincerely follows it, cannot dangerously err. If therefore the executive, who has the power of convoking the legislative, observing rather the true proportion, than fashion[4] of representation, regulates, not by old custom, but true reason, the number of members, in all places that have a right to be distinctly represented, which no part of the people however incorporated[5] can pretend to, but in proportion to the assistance which it affords to the public, it cannot be judged to have set up a new legislative, but to have restored the old and true one, and to have rectified the disorders which succession of time had insensibly, as well as inevitably introduced: For it being the interest as well as intention of the people, to have a fair and equal rep-

---

1 *flux*   State of change.
2 *sheepcote*   Small building for sheltering sheep.
3 *Salus populi suprema lex*   Latin: the welfare of the people is the supreme law.
4 *fashion*   Appearances.
5 *incorporated*   United into one body.

resentative; whoever brings it nearest to that, is an undoubted friend to, and establisher of the government, and cannot miss the consent and approbation of the community; prerogative being nothing but a power, in the hands of the prince, to provide for the public good, in such cases, which depending upon unforeseen and uncertain occurrences, certain and unalterable laws could not safely direct; whatsoever shall be done manifestly for the good of the people, and the establishing the government upon its true foundations, is, and always will be, just prerogative. The power of erecting new corporations,[1] and therewith new representatives, carries with it a supposition, that in time the measures of representation might vary, and those places have a just right to be represented which before had none; and by the same reason, those cease to have a right, and be too inconsiderable for such a privilege, which before had it. It is not a change from the present state, which perhaps corruption or decay has introduced, that makes an inroad upon the government, but the tendency of it to injure or oppress the people, and to set up one part or party, with a distinction from, and an unequal subjection of the rest. Whatsoever cannot but be acknowledged to be of advantage to the society, and people in general, upon just and lasting measures, will always, when done, justify itself; and whenever the people shall choose their representatives upon just and undeniably equal measures, suitable to the original frame of the government, it cannot be doubted to be the will and act of the society, whoever permitted or caused them so to do.

Chapter 14. Of Prerogative

§ 159. Where the legislative and executive power are in distinct hands, (as they are in all moderated[2] monarchies, and well-framed governments) there the good of the society requires, that several things should be left to the discretion of him that has the executive power: for the legislators not being able to foresee, and provide by laws, for all that may be useful to the community, the executor of the laws having the power in his hands, has by the common law of nature a right to make use of it for the good of the society, in many cases, where the municipal law has given no direction, till the legislative can conveniently be assembled to provide for it. Many things there are, which the law can by no means provide for; and those must necessarily be left to the discretion of him that has the executive power in his hands, to be ordered by him as the public good and advantage shall require: nay, it is fit that the

---

1 *corporations* Bodies of people united to act as collective entities.
2 *moderated* Not excessive, reasonable.

laws themselves should in some cases give way to the executive power, or rather to this fundamental law of nature and government, viz. That as much as may be,[1] all the members of the society are to be preserved: for since many accidents may happen, wherein a strict and rigid observation of the laws may do harm; (as not to pull down an innocent man's house to stop the fire, when the next to it is burning) and a man may come sometimes within the reach of the law, which makes no distinction of persons, by an action that may deserve reward and pardon; it is fit the ruler should have a power, in many cases, to mitigate the severity of the law, and pardon some offenders: for the end of government being the preservation of all, as much as may be, even the guilty are to be spared, where it can prove no prejudice to the innocent.

§ 160. This power to act according to discretion, for the public good, without the prescription of the law, and sometimes even against it, is that which is called prerogative: for since in some governments the lawmaking power is not always in being, and is usually too numerous, and so too slow, for the dispatch requisite to execution; and because also it is impossible to foresee, and so by laws to provide for, all accidents and necessities that may concern the public, or to make such laws as will do no harm, if they are executed with an inflexible rigor, on all occasions, and upon all persons that may come in their way; therefore there is a latitude left to the executive power, to do many things of choice which the laws do not prescribe.

§ 161. This power, while employed for the benefit of the community, and suitably to the trust and ends of the government, is undoubted prerogative, and never is questioned: for the people are very seldom or never scrupulous or nice[2] in the point; they are far from examining prerogative, while it is in any tolerable degree employed for the use it was meant, that is, for the good of the people, and not manifestly against it: but if there comes to be a question between the executive power and the people, about a thing claimed as a prerogative; the tendency of the exercise of such prerogative to the good or hurt of the people, will easily decide that question.

§ 162. It is easy to conceive, that in the infancy of governments, when commonwealths differed little from families in number of people, they differed from them too but little in number of laws: and the governors, being as the fathers of them, watching over them for their good, the government was almost all prerogative. A few established laws served the turn, and the discretion and care of the ruler supplied the rest. But when mistake or flattery prevailed with weak princes to

---

1   *as much as may be*   To the extent possible.
2   *nice*   Making subtle discriminations.

make use of this power for private ends of their own, and not for the public good, the people were fain[1] by express laws to get prerogative determined in those points wherein they found disadvantage from it: and thus declared limitations of prerogative were by the people found necessary in cases which they and their ancestors had left, in the utmost latitude, to the wisdom of those princes who made no other but a right use of it, that is, for the good of their people.

§ 163. And therefore they have a very wrong notion of government, who say, that the people have encroached upon the prerogative, when they have got any part of it to be defined by positive laws: for in so doing they have not pulled from the prince any thing that of right belonged to him, but only declared, that that power which they indefinitely left in his or his ancestors' hands, to be exercised for their good, was not a thing which they intended him when he used it otherwise: for the end of government being the good of the community, whatsoever alterations are made in it, tending to that end, cannot be an encroachment upon anybody, since nobody in government can have a right tending to any other end: and those only are encroachments which prejudice or hinder the public good. Those who say otherwise, speak as if the prince had a distinct and separate interest from the good of the community, and was not made for it; the root and source from which spring almost all those evils and disorders which happen in kingly governments. And indeed, if that be so, the people under his government are not a society of rational creatures, entered into a community for their mutual good; they are not such as have set rulers over themselves, to guard, and promote that good; but are to be looked on as an herd of inferior creatures under the dominion of a master, who keeps them and works them for his own pleasure or profit. If men were so void of reason, and brutish, as to enter into society upon such terms, prerogative might indeed be, what some men would have it, an arbitrary power to do things hurtful to the people.

§ 164. But since a rational creature cannot be supposed, when free, to put himself into subjection to another, for his own harm; (though, where he finds a good and wise ruler, he may not perhaps think it either necessary or useful to set precise bounds to his power in all things) prerogative can be nothing but the people's permitting their rulers to do several things, of their own free choice, where the law was silent, and sometimes too against the direct letter of the law, for the public good; and their acquiescing in it when so done: for as a good prince, who is mindful of the trust put into his hands, and careful of the good of his people, cannot have too much prerogative, that is, power to do

---

1   *fain*   Glad under the circumstances.

good; so a weak and ill prince, who would claim that power which his predecessors exercised without the direction of the law, as a prerogative belonging to him by right of his office, which he may exercise at his pleasure, to make or promote an interest distinct from that of the public, gives the people an occasion to claim their right, and limit that power, which, while it was exercised for their good, they were content should be tacitly allowed.

§ 165. And therefore he that will look into the history of England, will find, that prerogative was always largest in the hands of our wisest and best princes; because the people, observing the whole tendency of their actions to be the public good, contested not what was done without law to that end: or, if any human frailty or mistake (for princes are but men, made as others) appeared in some small declinations[1] from that end; yet it was visible, the main of their conduct tended to nothing but the care of the public. The people therefore, finding reason to be satisfied with these princes, whenever they acted without, or contrary to the letter of the law, acquiesced in what they did, and, without the least complaint, let them enlarge their prerogative as they pleased, judging rightly, that they did nothing herein to the prejudice of their laws, since they acted conformable to the foundation and end of all laws, the public good.

§ 166. Such godlike princes indeed had some title to arbitrary power by that argument, that would prove absolute monarchy the best government, as that which God himself governs the universe by; because such kings partake of his wisdom and goodness. Upon this is founded that saying, That the reigns of good princes have been always most dangerous to the liberties of their people: for when their successors, managing the government with different thoughts, would draw the actions of those good rulers into precedent, and make them the standard of their prerogative, as if what had been done only for the good of the people was a right in them to do, for the harm of the people, if they so pleased; it has often occasioned contest,[2] and sometimes public disorders, before the people could recover their original right, and get that to be declared not to be prerogative, which truly was never so; since it is impossible that anybody in the society should ever have a right to do the people harm; though it be very possible, and reasonable, that the people should not go about to set any bounds to the prerogative of those kings, or rulers, who themselves transgressed not the bounds of the public good: for prerogative is nothing but the power of doing public good without a rule.

---

1 *declinations* Deviations.
2 *contest* Struggle for control.

§ 167. The power of calling parliaments in England, as to precise time, place, and duration, is certainly a prerogative of the king, but still with this trust, that it shall be made use of for the good of the nation, as the exigencies of the times, and variety of occasions, shall require: for it being impossible to foresee which should always be the fittest place for them to assemble in, and what the best season; the choice of these was left with the executive power, as might be most subservient to the public good, and best suit the ends of parliaments.

§ 168. The old question will be asked in this matter of prerogative, But who shall be judge when this power is made a right use of? I answer: between an executive power in being,[1] with such a prerogative, and a legislative that depends upon his will for their convening, there can be no judge on earth; as there can be none between the legislative and the people, should either the executive, or the legislative, when they have got the power in their hands, design, or go about to enslave or destroy them. The people have no other remedy in this, as in all other cases where they have no judge on earth, but to appeal to heaven: for the rulers, in such attempts, exercising a power the people never put into their hands, (who can never be supposed to consent that anybody should rule over them for their harm) do that which they have not a right to do. And where the body of the people, or any single man, is deprived of their right, or is under the exercise of a power without right, and have no appeal on earth, then they have a liberty to appeal to heaven, whenever they judge the cause of sufficient moment. And therefore, though the people cannot be judge, so as to have, by the constitution of that society, any superior power, to determine and give effective sentence in the case; yet they have, by a law antecedent and paramount to all positive laws of men, reserved that ultimate determination to themselves which belongs to all mankind, where there lies no appeal on earth, viz. to judge, whether they have just cause to make their appeal to heaven. And this judgment they cannot part with, it being out of a man's power so to submit himself to another, as to give him a liberty to destroy him; God and nature never allowing a man so to abandon himself, as to neglect his own preservation: and since he cannot take away his own life, neither can he give another power to take it. Nor let anyone think, this lays a perpetual foundation for disorder; for this operates not, till the inconveniency is so great, that the majority feel it, and are weary of it, and find a necessity to have it amended. But this the executive power, or wise princes, never need come in the danger of: and it is the thing, of all others, they have most need to avoid, as of all others the most perilous.

---

1   *in being*   In existence.

Chapter 15. Of Paternal, Political, and Despotical Power, considered together

§ 169. Though I have had occasion to speak of these separately before, yet the great mistakes of late about government, having, as I suppose, arisen from confounding these distinct powers one with another, it may not, perhaps, be amiss to consider them here together.

§ 170. First, then, Paternal or parental power is nothing but that which parents have over their children, to govern them for the children's good, till they come to the use of reason, or a state of knowledge, wherein they may be supposed capable to understand that rule, whether it be the law of nature, or the municipal law of their country, they are to govern themselves by: capable, I say, to know it, as well as several others, who live as freemen under that law. The affection and tenderness which God has planted in the breast of parents towards their children, makes it evident, that this is not intended to be a severe arbitrary government, but only for the help, instruction, and preservation of their offspring. But happen it as it will,[1] there is, as I have proved, no reason why it should be thought to extend to life and death, at any time, over their children, more than over anybody else; neither can there be any pretense[2] why this parental power should keep the child, when grown to a man, in subjection to the will of his parents, any farther than having received life and education from his parents, obliges him to respect, honor, gratitude, assistance and support, all his life, to both father and mother. And thus, it is true, the paternal is a natural government, but not at all extending itself to the ends and jurisdictions of that which is political. The power of the father does not reach at all to the property of the child, which is only in his own disposing.

§ 171. Secondly, Political power is that power, which every man having in the state of nature, has given up into the hands of the society, and therein to the governors, whom the society has set over itself, with this express or tacit trust, that it shall be employed for their good, and the preservation of their property: now this power, which every man has in the state of nature, and which he parts with to the society in all such cases where the society can secure him, is to use such means, for the preserving of his own property, as he thinks good, and nature allows him; and to punish the breach of the law of nature in others, so as (according to the best of his reason) may most conduce[3]

---

1 *happen it as it will*   That is, however individual families manage this.
2 *pretense*   Unwarranted claim.
3 *conduce*   Contribute.

to the preservation of himself, and the rest of mankind. So that the end and measure of this power, when in every man's hands in the state of nature, being the preservation of all of his society, that is, all mankind in general, it can have no other end or measure, when in the hands of the magistrate, but to preserve the members of that society in their lives, liberties, and possessions; and so cannot be an absolute, arbitrary power over their lives and fortunes, which are as much as possible to be preserved; but a power to make laws, and annex such penalties to them, as may tend to the preservation of the whole, by cutting off those parts, and those only, which are so corrupt, that they threaten the sound and healthy, without which no severity is lawful. And this power has its original only from compact and agreement, and the mutual consent of those who make up the community.

§ 172. Thirdly, Despotical power is an absolute, arbitrary power one man has over another, to take away his life, whenever he pleases. This is a power, which neither nature gives, for it has made no such distinction betwixt one man and another; nor compact can convey: for man not having such an arbitrary power over his own life, cannot give another man such a power over it; but it is the effect only of forfeiture, which the aggressor makes of his own life, when he puts himself into the state of war with another: for having quitted reason,[1] which God has given to be the rule between man and man, and the common bond whereby human kind is united into one fellowship and society; and having renounced the way of peace which that teaches, and made use of the force of war, to compass his unjust ends upon another, where he has no right; and so revolting from his own kind to that of beasts, by making force, which is theirs, to be his rule of right, he renders himself liable to be destroyed by the injured person, and the rest of mankind, that will join with him in the execution of justice, as any other wild beast, or noxious brute, with whom mankind can have neither society nor security.[2] And thus captives, taken in a just and lawful war, and such only, are subject to a despotical power, which, as it arises not from compact, so neither is it capable of any, but is the state of war continued: for what compact can be made with a man that is not master of his own life? what condition can he perform? and if he be once allowed to be master of his own life, the despotical, arbitrary power of his master ceases. He that is master of himself, and his own life, has a right too to the means of preserving it; so that as soon as

---

1   *quitted reason*   Stopped being rational.

2   *and so revolting ... society nor security*   [note in original publication] Another copy corrected by Mr. Locke, has it thus, "Noxious brute that is destructive to their being."

compact enters, slavery ceases, and he so far quits his absolute power, and puts an end to the state of war, who enters into conditions with his captive.

§ 173. Nature gives the first of these, viz. paternal power to parents for the benefit of their children during their minority, to supply their want of ability, and understanding how to manage their property. (By property I must be understood here, as in other places, to mean that property which men have in their persons as well as goods.) Voluntary agreement gives the second, viz. political power to governors for the benefit of their subjects, to secure them in the possession and use of their properties. And forfeiture gives the third despotical power to lords for their own benefit, over those who are stripped of all property.

§ 174. He, that shall consider the distinct rise and extent, and the different ends of these several powers, will plainly see, that paternal power comes as far short of that of the magistrate, as despotical exceeds it; and that absolute dominion, however placed, is so far from being one kind of civil society, that it is as inconsistent with it, as slavery is with property. Paternal power is only where minority makes the child incapable to manage his property; political, where men have property in their own disposal; and despotical, over such as have no property at all.

Chapter 16. Of Conquest

§ 175. Though governments can originally have no other rise than that before mentioned, nor polities be founded on any thing but the consent of the people; yet such have been the disorders ambition has filled the world with, that in the noise of war, which makes so great a part of the history of mankind, this consent is little taken notice of: and therefore many have mistaken the force of arms for the consent of the people, and reckon conquest as one of the originals of government. But conquest is as far from setting up any government, as demolishing an house is from building a new one in the place. Indeed, it often makes way for a new frame of a commonwealth, by destroying the former; but, without the consent of the people, can never erect a new one.

§ 176. That the aggressor, who puts himself into the state of war with another, and unjustly invades another man's right, can, by such an unjust war, never come to have a right over the conquered, will be easily agreed by all men, who will not think, that robbers and pirates have a right of empire over whomsoever they have force enough to master; or that men are bound by promises, which unlawful force extorts from them. Should a robber break into my house, and with a dagger at my throat make me seal deeds to convey my estate to him, would this give him any title? Just such a title, by his sword, has an unjust conqueror, who forces me into submission. The injury and the crime is equal, whether committed by the wearer of a crown, or some petty villain. The title of the offender, and the number of his followers, make no difference in the offence, unless it be to aggravate it. The only difference is, great robbers punish little ones, to keep them in their obedience; but the great ones are rewarded with laurels[1] and triumphs,[2] because they are too big for the weak hands of justice in this world, and have the power in their own possession, which should punish offenders. What is my remedy against a robber, that so broke into my house? Appeal to the law for justice. But perhaps justice is denied, or I am crippled and cannot stir, robbed and have not the means to do it. If God has taken away all means of seeking remedy, there is nothing left but patience.[3] But my son, when able, may seek the relief of the law, which I am denied: he or his son may renew his appeal, till he recover his right. But the conquered, or their children, have no court, no arbitrator on earth to appeal to. Then they may appeal, as Jephtha did, to heaven, and repeat their appeal till they have recovered the native right of their ancestors, which was, to have such a legislative over them, as the majority should approve, and freely acquiesce in. If it be objected, This would cause endless trouble; I answer, no more than justice does, where she lies open to all that appeal to her. He that troubles his neighbor without a cause, is punished for it by the justice of the court he appeals to: and he that appeals to heaven must be sure he has right on his side; and a right too that is worth the trouble and cost of the appeal, as he will answer at a tribunal that cannot be deceived, and will be sure to retribute to everyone according to the mischiefs he has created to his fellow subjects; that is, any part of mankind: from whence it is plain, that he that conquers in an unjust war can thereby have no title to the subjection and obedience of the conquered.

§ 177. But supposing victory favors the right side, let us consider a conqueror in a lawful war, and see what power he gets, and over whom.

First, It is plain he gets no power by his conquest over those that conquered with him. They that fought on his side cannot suffer by the conquest, but must at least be as much freemen as they were before. And most commonly they serve upon terms,[4] and on condition to share with their leader, and enjoy a part of the spoil, and other advantages

---

1   *laurels*   Wreath of leaves, ancient symbol of victory.
2   *triumphs*   Ancient Roman victory parade.
3   *patience*   Calm endurance.
4   *upon terms*   By agreement.

that attend the conquering sword; or at least have a part of the subdued country bestowed upon them. And the conquering people are not,
I hope, to be slaves by conquest, and wear their laurels only to show
they are sacrifices to their leaders' triumph. They that found absolute
monarchy upon the title of the sword, make their heroes, who are the
founders of such monarchies, arrant Draw-can-sirs,[1] and forget they
had any officers and soldiers that fought on their side in the battles
they won, or assisted them in the subduing, or shared in possessing, the
countries they mastered. We are told by some, that the English monarchy is founded in the Norman conquest, and that our princes have
thereby a title to absolute dominion: which if it were true, (as by the
history it appears otherwise) and that William[2] had a right to make war
on this island; yet his dominion by conquest could reach no farther
than to the Saxons and Britons, that were then inhabitants of this country. The Normans that came with him, and helped to conquer, and all
descended from them, are freemen, and no subjects by conquest; let
that give what dominion it will. And if I, or anybody else, shall claim
freedom, as derived from them, it will be very hard to prove the contrary: and it is plain, the law, that has made no distinction between the
one and the other, intends not there should be any difference in their
freedom or privileges.

§ 178. But supposing, which seldom happens, that the conquerors
and conquered never incorporate into one people, under the same laws
and freedom; let us see next what power a lawful conqueror has over
the subdued: and that I say is purely despotical. He has an absolute
power over the lives of those who by an unjust war have forfeited
them; but not over the lives or fortunes of those who engaged not in
the war, nor over the possessions even of those who were actually engaged in it.

§ 179. Secondly, I say then the conqueror gets no power but only
over those who have actually assisted, concurred, or consented to that
unjust force that is used against him: for the people having given to
their governors no power to do an unjust thing, such as is to make an
unjust war, (for they never had such a power in themselves) they ought
not to be charged as guilty of the violence and injustice that is committed in an unjust war, any farther than they actually abet it;[3] no more
than they are to be thought guilty of any violence or oppression their

---

1 *Draw-can-sirs* Drawcansir is a blustering braggart and bully in a 1672 play by
   George Villiers called *The Rehearsal*.

2 *William* William the Conqueror, the first Norman king of England, who reigned
   from 1066 until his death in 1087.

3 *abet it* Help them do it.

governors should use upon the people themselves, or any part of their fellow subjects, they having empowered them no more to the one than to the other. Conquerors, it is true, seldom trouble themselves to make the distinction, but they willingly permit the confusion of war to sweep all together: but yet this alters not the right; for the conquerors power over the lives of the conquered, being only because they have used force to do, or maintain an injustice, he can have that power only over those who have concurred in that force; all the rest are innocent; and he has no more title over the people of that country, who have done him no injury, and so have made no forfeiture of their lives, than he has over any other, who, without any injuries or provocations, have lived upon fair terms with him.

§ 180. Thirdly, The power a conqueror gets over those he overcomes in a just war, is perfectly despotical: he has an absolute power over the lives of those, who, by putting themselves in a state of war, have forfeited them; but he has not thereby a right and title to their possessions. This I doubt not, but at first sight will seem a strange doctrine, it being so quite contrary to the practice of the world; there being nothing more familiar in speaking of the dominion of countries, than to say such an one conquered it; as if conquest, without any more ado, conveyed a right of possession. But when we consider, that the practice of the strong and powerful, however universal it may be, is seldom the rule of right, however it be one part of the subjection of the conquered, not to argue against the conditions cut out to them by the conquering sword.

§ 181. Though in all war there be usually a complication[1] of force and damage, and the aggressor seldom fails to harm the estate, when he uses force against the persons of those he makes war upon; yet it is the use of force only that puts a man into the state of war: for whether by force he begins the injury, or else having quietly, and by fraud, done the injury, he refuses to make reparation, and by force maintains it, (which is the same thing, as at first to have done it by force) it is the unjust use of force that makes the war: for he that breaks open my house, and violently turns me out of doors; or having peaceably got in, by force keeps me out, does in effect the same thing; supposing we are in such a state, that we have no common judge on earth, whom I may appeal to, and to whom we are both obliged to submit: for of such I am now speaking. It is the unjust use of force then, that puts a man into the state of war with another; and thereby he that is guilty of it makes a forfeiture of his life: for quitting reason, which is the rule given between man and man, and using force, the way of beasts, he be-

---

1   *complication*   Tangled combination.

comes liable to be destroyed by him he uses force against, as any savage ravenous beast, that is dangerous to his being.

§ 182. But because the miscarriages of the father are no faults of the children, and they may be rational and peaceable, notwithstanding the brutishness and injustice of the father; the father, by his miscarriages and violence, can forfeit but his own life, but involves not his children in his guilt or destruction. His goods, which nature, that wills the preservation of all mankind as much as is possible, has made to belong to the children to keep them from perishing, do still continue to belong to his children: for supposing them not to have joined in the war, either through infancy, absence, or choice, they have done nothing to forfeit them: nor has the conqueror any right to take them away, by the bare title of having subdued him that by force attempted his destruction; though perhaps he may have some right to them, to repair the damages he has sustained by the war, and the defense of his own right; which how far it reaches to the possessions of the conquered, we shall see by and by. So that he that by conquest has a right over a man's person to destroy him if he pleases, has not thereby a right over his estate to possess and enjoy it: for it is the brutal force the aggressor has used, that gives his adversary a right to take away his life, and destroy him if he pleases, as a noxious creature; but it is damage sustained that alone gives him title to another man's goods: for though I may kill a thief that sets on me in the highway, yet I may not (which seems less) take away his money, and let him go: this would be robbery on my side. His force, and the state of war he put himself in, made him forfeit his life, but gave me no title to his goods. The right then of conquest extends only to the lives of those who joined in the war, not to their estates, but only in order to make reparation for the damages received, and the charges of the war, and that too with reservation of the right of the innocent wife and children.

§ 183. Let the conqueror have as much justice on his side, as could be supposed, he has no right to seize more than the vanquished could forfeit: his life is at the victor's mercy; and his service and goods he may appropriate, to make himself reparation; but he cannot take the goods of his wife and children; they too had a title to the goods he enjoyed, and their shares in the estate he possessed: for example, I in the state of nature (and all commonwealths are in the state of nature one with another) have injured another man, and refusing to give satisfaction, it comes to a state of war, wherein my defending by force what I had gotten unjustly, makes me the aggressor. I am conquered: my life, it is true, as forfeit, is at mercy, but not my wife's and children's. They made not the war, nor assisted in it. I could not forfeit their lives; they were not mine to forfeit. My wife had a share in my estate; that neither could I forfeit. And my children also, being born of me, had a right to be maintained out of my labor or substance.[1] Here then is the case: the conqueror has a title[2] to reparation for damages received, and the children have a title to their father's estate for their subsistence: for as to the wife's share, whether her own labor, or compact, gave her a title to it, it is plain, her husband could not forfeit what was hers. What must be done in the case? I answer; the fundamental law of nature being, that all, as much as may be, should be preserved, it follows, that if there be not enough fully to satisfy both, viz, for the conqueror's losses, and children's maintenance, he that has, and to spare, must remit something of his full satisfaction, and give way to the pressing and preferable title of those who are in danger to perish without it.

§ 184. But supposing the charge and damages of the war are to be made up to the conqueror, to the utmost farthing; and that the children of the vanquished, spoiled of all their father's goods, are to be left to starve and perish; yet the satisfying of what shall, on this score, be due to the conqueror, will scarce give him a title to any country he shall conquer: for the damages of war can scarce amount to the value of any considerable tract of land, in any part of the world, where all the land is possessed, and none lies waste. And if I have not taken away the conqueror's land, which, being vanquished, it is impossible I should; scarce any other spoil I have done him[3] can amount to the value of mine, supposing it equally cultivated, and of an extent any way coming near what I had overrun of his. The destruction of a year's product or two (for it seldom reaches four or five) is the utmost spoil that usually can be done: for as to money, and such riches and treasure taken away, these are none of nature's goods, they have but a fantastical[4] imaginary value: nature has put no such upon them: they are of no more account by her standard, than the wampompeke[5] of the Americans to an European prince, or the silver money of Europe would have been formerly to an American. And five years product is not worth the perpetual inheritance of land, where all is possessed, and none remains waste, to be taken up by him that is deceased: which will be easily granted, if one do but take away the imaginary value of money, the disproportion being more than between five and five hundred; though, at the same time, half a year's product is more worth than the inheritance, where there being more land than the inhabitants possess and make use of, anyone has liberty to make use of the waste: but there

---

1   *substance*   Possessions.
2   *title*   Right.
3   *spoil I have done him*   Property of his I have destroyed or taken.
4   *fantastical*   In fantasy—unreal.
5   *wampompeke*   "Wampum"—money of the North American aboriginal peoples.

conquerors take little care to possess themselves of the lands of the vanquished. No damage therefore, that men in the state of nature (as all princes and governments are in reference to one another) suffer from one another, can give a conqueror power to dispossess the posterity of the vanquished, and turn them out of that inheritance, which ought to be the possession of them and their descendants to all generations. The conqueror indeed will be apt to think himself master: and it is the very condition of the subdued not to be able to dispute their right. But if that be all, it gives no other title than what bare force gives to the stronger over the weaker: and, by this reason, he that is strongest will have a right to whatever he pleases to seize on.

§ 185. Over those then that joined with him in the war, and over those of the subdued country that opposed him not, and the posterity even of those that did, the conqueror, even in a just war, has, by his conquest, no right of dominion: they are free from any subjection to him, and if their former government be dissolved, they are at liberty to begin and erect another to themselves.

§ 186. The conqueror, it is true, usually, by the force he has over them, compels them, with a sword at their breasts, to stoop to his conditions, and submit to such a government as he pleases to afford them; but the enquiry is, what right he has to do so? If it be said, they submit by their own consent, then this allows their own consent to be necessary to give the conqueror a title to rule over them. It remains only to be considered, whether promises extorted by force, without right, can be thought consent, and how far they bind. To which I shall say, they bind not at all; because whatsoever another gets from me by force, I still retain the right of, and he is obliged presently to restore. He that forces my horse from me, ought presently to restore him, and I have still a right to retake him. By the same reason, he that forced a promise from me, ought presently to restore it, i.e., quit me of the obligation of it; or I may resume it myself, i.e., choose whether I will perform it: for the law of nature laying an obligation on me only by the rules she[1] prescribes, cannot oblige me by the violation of her rules: such is the extorting any thing from me by force. Nor does it at all alter the case to say, I gave my promise, no more than it excuses the force, and passes the right, when I put my hand in my pocket, and deliver my purse myself to a thief, who demands it with a pistol at my breast.

§ 187. From all which it follows, that the government of a conqueror, imposed by force on the subdued, against whom he had no right of war, or who joined not in the war against him, where he had right, has no obligation upon them.

---

1 *she* Nature.

§ 188. But let us suppose, that all the men of that community, being all members of the same body politic, may be taken to have joined in that unjust war wherein they are subdued, and so their lives are at the mercy of the conqueror.

§ 189. I say, this concerns not their children who are in their minority: for since a father has not, in himself, a power over the life or liberty of his child, no act of his can possibly forfeit it. So that the children, whatever may have happened to the fathers, are freemen, and the absolute power of the conqueror reaches no farther than the persons of the men that were subdued by him, and dies with them: and should he govern them as slaves, subjected to his absolute arbitrary power, he has no such right of dominion over their children. He can have no power over them but by their own consent, whatever he may drive them to say or do; and he has no lawful authority, while force, and not choice, compels them to submission.

§ 190. Every man is born with a double right: first, a right of freedom to his person, which no other man has a power over, but the free disposal of it lies in himself. Secondly, a right, before any other man, to inherit with his brethren his father's goods.

§ 191. By the first of these, a man is naturally free from subjection to any government, though he be born in a place under its jurisdiction; but if he disclaim the lawful government of the country he was born in, he must also quit the right that belonged to him by the laws of it, and the possessions there descending to him from his ancestors, if it were a government made by their consent.

§ 192. By the second, the inhabitants of any country, who are descended, and derive a title to their estates from those who are subdued, and had a government forced upon them against their free consents, retain a right to the possession of their ancestors, though they consent not freely to the government, whose hard conditions were by force imposed on the possessors of that country: for the first conqueror never having had a title to the land of that country, the people who are the descendants of, or claim under those who were forced to submit to the yoke of a government by constraint, have always a right to shake it off, and free themselves from the usurpation or tyranny which the sword has brought in upon them, till their rulers put them under such a frame of government as they willingly and of choice consent to. Who doubts but the Grecian Christians, descendants of the ancient possessors of that country, may justly cast off the Turkish yoke,[1] which they have so long groaned under, whenever they have an opportunity to do

---

1   *Grecian Christians ... Turkish yoke*   Christian Greece was ruled by the Ottoman Empire (i.e., by Turkish Muslims) since the 15th century, and until 1821.

it? For no government can have a right to obedience from a people who have not freely consented to it; which they can never be supposed to do, till either they are put in a full state of liberty to choose their government and governors, or at least till they have such standing laws, to which they have by themselves or their representatives given their free consent, and also till they are allowed their due property, which is so to be proprietors of what they have, that nobody can take away any part of it without their own consent, without which, men under any government are not in the state of freemen, but are direct slaves under the force of war.

§ 193. But granting that the conqueror in a just war has a right to the estates, as well as power over the persons, of the conquered; which, it is plain, he has not:[1] nothing of absolute power will follow from hence, in the continuance of the government; because the descendants of these being all freemen, if he grants them estates and possessions to inhabit his country, (without which it would be worth nothing) whatsoever he grants them, they have, so far as it is granted, property in. The nature whereof is, that without a man's own consent it cannot be taken from him.

§ 194. Their persons are free by a native[2] right, and their properties, be they more or less, are their own, and at their own dispose,[3] and not at his; or else it is no property. Supposing the conqueror gives to one man a thousand acres, to him and his heirs forever; to another he lets[4] a thousand acres for his life, under the rent of 50 pounds or 500 pounds per annum, has not the one of these a right to his thousand acres forever, and the other, during his life, paying the said rent? and has not the tenant for life a property in all that he gets over and above his rent, by his labor and industry during the said term, supposing it be double the rent? Can anyone say, the king, or conqueror, after his grant, may by his power of conqueror take away all, or part of the land from the heirs of one, or from the other during his life, he paying the rent? or can he take away from either the goods or money they have got upon the said land, at his pleasure? If he can, then all free and voluntary contracts cease, and are void in the world; there needs nothing to dissolve them at any time, but power enough: and all the grants and promises of men in power are but mockery and collusion:[5] for can there be any thing more ridiculous than to say, I give you and yours this forever, and that

---

1 *But granting ... he has not* Locke means here: Even supposing that the conquerer ... had a right ... —which he plainly does not.

2 *native* Inborn, natural.

3 *at their own dispose* To be dealt with by their own choice.

4 *lets* Rents.

5 *collusion* Secret fraudulent agreement.

in the surest and most solemn way of conveyance can be devised; and yet it is to be understood, that I have right, if I please, to take it away from you again tomorrow?

§ 195. I will not dispute now whether princes are exempt from the laws of their country; but this I am sure, they owe subjection to the laws of God and nature. Nobody, no power, can exempt them from the obligations of that eternal law. Those are so great, and so strong, in the case of promises, that omnipotency[1] itself can be tied by them. Grants, promises, and oaths, are bonds that hold the Almighty: whatever some flatterers say to princes of the world, who all together, with all their people joined to them, are, in comparison of the great God, but as a drop of the bucket, or a dust on the balance, inconsiderable, nothing!

§ 196. The short of the case in conquest is this: the conqueror, if he have a just cause, has a despotical right over the persons of all, that actually aided, and concurred in the war against him, and a right to make up his damage and cost out of their labor and estates, so he injure not the right of any other. Over the rest of the people, if there were any that consented not to the war, and over the children of the captives themselves, or the possessions of either, he has no power; and so can have, by virtue of conquest, no lawful title himself to dominion over them, or derive it to his posterity; but is an aggressor, if he attempts upon their properties, and thereby puts himself in a state of war against them, and has no better a right of principality, he, nor any of his successors, than Hingar, or Hubba, the Danes, had here in England;[2] or Spartacus,[3] had he conquered Italy, would have had; which is to have their yoke cast off, as soon as God shall give those under their subjection courage and opportunity to do it. Thus, notwithstanding whatever title the kings of Assyria had over Judah, by the sword, God assisted Hezekiah to throw off the dominion of that conquering empire. "And the lord was with Hezekiah, and he prospered; wherefore he went forth, and he rebelled against the king of Assyria, and served him not" (2 Kings xviii. 7). Whence it is plain, that shaking off a power, which force, and not right, has set over anyone, though it has the name of rebellion, yet is no offence before God, but is that which he allows and countenances, though even promises and covenants, when obtained by force, have intervened: for it is very probable, to anyone that reads

---

1   omnipotency   The state of being all-powerful, infinitely powerful.
2   Hingar, or Hubba ... in England   Most likely a reference to Ingware and Ubba, leaders of the Norse army that invaded England during the 860s.
3   Spartacus   Gladiator-slave who led a slave rebellion against Rome, defeated in 71 BCE.

the story of Ahaz and Hezekiah attentively, that the Assyrians subdued Ahaz, and deposed him, and made Hezekiah king in his father's lifetime; and that Hezekiah by agreement had done him homage, and paid him tribute all this time.

Chapter 17. Of Usurpation

§ 197. As conquest may be called a foreign usurpation, so usurpation is a kind of domestic conquest, with this difference, that an usurper can never have right on his side, it being no usurpation, but where one is got into the possession of what another has right to.[1] This, so far as it is usurpation, is a change only of persons, but not of the forms and rules of the government: for if the usurper extend his power beyond what of right belonged to the lawful princes, or governors of the commonwealth, it is tyranny added to usurpation.

§ 198. In all lawful governments, the designation of the persons, who are to bear rule, is as natural and necessary a part as the form of the government itself, and is that which had its establishment originally from the people; the anarchy being much alike, to have no form of government at all, or to agree that it shall be monarchical, but to appoint no way to design the person that shall have the power, and be the monarch. Hence all commonwealths, with the form of government established, have rules also of appointing those who are to have any share in the public authority, and settled methods of conveying the right to them. Whoever gets into the exercise of any part of the power, by other ways than what the laws of the community have prescribed, has no right to be obeyed, though the form of the commonwealth be still preserved; since he is not the person the laws have appointed, and consequently not the person the people have consented to. Nor can such an usurper, or any deriving from him, ever have a title, till the people are both at liberty to consent, and have actually consented to allow, and confirm in him the power he has till then usurped.

Chapter 18. Of Tyranny

§ 199. As usurpation is the exercise of power, which another has a right to; so tyranny is the exercise of power beyond right, which nobody can have a right to. And this is making use of the power anyone has in his hands, not for the good of those who are under it, but for his own private separate advantage. When the governor, however entitled,

---

1   *it being no usurpation ... another has right to*   Locke means: It is not usurpation when one has the right to what one gets.

makes not the law, but his will, the rule; and his commands and actions are not directed to the preservation of the properties of his people, but the satisfaction of his own ambition, revenge, covetousness, or any other irregular passion.

§ 200. If one can doubt this to be truth, or reason, because it comes from the obscure hand of a subject, I hope the authority of a king will make it pass with him. King James the First, in his speech to the parliament, 1603, tells them thus,

I will ever prefer the weal of the public, and of the whole commonwealth, in making of good laws and constitutions, to any particular and private ends of mine; thinking ever the wealth and weal[1] of the commonwealth to be my greatest weal and worldly felicity; a point wherein a lawful king doth directly differ from a tyrant: for I do acknowledge, that the special and greatest point of difference that is betwixt a rightful king and an usurping tyrant, is this, that whereas the proud and ambitious tyrant doth think his kingdom and people are only ordained for satisfaction of his desires and unreasonable appetites, the righteous and just king doth by the contrary acknowledge himself to be ordained for the procuring of the wealth and property of his people.

And again, in his speech to the parliament, 1609, he had these words:

The king binds himself by a double oath, to the observation of the fundamental laws of his kingdom; tacitly, as by being a king, and so bound to protect as well the people, as the laws of his kingdom; and expressly, by his oath at his coronation, so as every just king, in a settled kingdom, is bound to observe that paction[2] made to his people, by his laws, in framing his government agreeable thereunto, according to that paction which God made with Noah after the deluge "Hereafter, seed-time and harvest, and cold and heat, and summer and winter, and day and night, shall not cease while the earth remaineth."[3] And therefore a king governing in a settled kingdom, leaves to be a king, and degenerates into a tyrant, as soon as he leaves off to rule according to his laws.

---

1   *wealth and weal*   Both these words can mean *material riches*; but in an older use (incorporated into the words 'commonwealth' and 'commonweal') both mean *well-being* or *happiness*.

2   *paction*   Agreement.

3   Genesis 8:22.

And a little after:

Therefore all kings that are not tyrants, or perjured, will be glad to bound themselves within the limits of their laws; and they that persuade them the contrary, are vipers, and pests both against them and the commonwealth. Thus that learned king, who well understood the notion of things, makes the difference between a king and a tyrant to consist only in this, that one makes the laws the bounds of his power, and the good of the public, the end of his government; the other makes all give way to his own will and appetite.

§ 201. It is a mistake, to think this fault is proper only to monarchies; other forms of government are liable to it, as well as that: for wherever the power, that is put in any hands for the government of the people, and the preservation of their properties, is applied to other ends, and made use of to impoverish, harass, or subdue them to the arbitrary and irregular commands of those that have it; there it presently becomes tyranny, whether those that thus use it are one or many. Thus we read of the thirty tyrants[1] at Athens, as well as one at Syracuse;[2] and the intolerable dominion of the Decemviri[3] at Rome was nothing better.

§ 202. Wherever law ends, tyranny begins, if the law be transgressed to another's harm; and whosoever in authority exceeds the power given him by the law, and makes use of the force he has under his command, to compass that upon the subject, which the law allows not,[4] ceases in that to be a magistrate; and, acting without authority, may be opposed, as any other man, who by force invades the right of another. This is acknowledged in subordinate magistrates. He that has authority to seize my person in the street, may be opposed as a thief and a robber, if he endeavors to break into my house to execute a

---

1 *thirty tyrants* Ruling group installed after Athens's defeat in the Peloponnesian War in 404 BCE. They disregarded their assignment (to draft a new constitution), abused their power, and killed off their opponents, confiscating their possessions.

2 *one at Syracuse* Opinions differ about which ruler of Syracuse (in Sicily) Locke meant here. Perhaps Dionysius I, also known as Dionysius the Elder (430-367 BCE), perhaps Agathocles (361?-289 BCE); both were known for their cruelty.

3 *Decemviri* Latin: ten men. There were various ten-man groups in ancient Rome, but Locke here refers to the group of magistrates (lawgivers) appointed with strong powers in 451 BCE; they became increasingly violent and tyrannical, refusing to leave at the end of their term, but they were forced out by an uprising afterwards.

4 *compass ... law allows not* Do to the subject that which the law does not allow.

writ,[1] notwithstanding that I know he has such a warrant, and such a legal authority, as will empower him to arrest me abroad.[2] And why this should not hold in the highest, as well as in the most inferior magistrate, I would gladly be informed. Is it reasonable, that the eldest brother, because he has the greatest part of his father's estate, should thereby have a right to take away any of his younger brothers' portions? or that a rich man, who possessed a whole country, should from thence have a right to seize, when he pleased, the cottage and garden of his poor neighbor? The being rightfully possessed of great power and riches, exceedingly beyond the greatest part of the sons of Adam, is so far from being an excuse, much less a reason, for rapine[3] and oppression, which the endamaging[4] another without authority is, that it is a great aggravation of it:[5] for the exceeding the bounds of authority is no more a right in a great, than in a petty officer; no more justifiable in a king than a constable; but is so much the worse in him, in that he has more trust put in him, has already a much greater share than the rest of his brethren, and is supposed, from the advantages of his education, employment, and counselors, to be more knowing in the measures of right and wrong.

§ 203. May the commands then of a prince be opposed? may he be resisted as often as anyone shall find himself aggrieved, and but imagine he has not right done him? This will unhinge and overturn all polities, and, instead of government and order, leave nothing but anarchy and confusion.

§ 204. To this I answer, that force is to be opposed to nothing, but to unjust and unlawful force; whoever makes any opposition in any other case, draws on himself a just condemnation both from God and man; and so no such danger or confusion will follow, as is often suggested: for,

§ 205. First, As, in some countries, the person of the prince by the law[6] is sacred; and so, whatever he commands or does, his person is still free from all question or violence, not liable to force, or any judicial censure or condemnation. But yet opposition may be made to the illegal acts of any inferior officer, or other commissioned by him; un-

---

1   *execute a writ*   Carry out the provisions of a legal order.
2   *abroad*   Outside (my house).
3   *rapine*   Illicit seizing of another's property.
4   *endamaging*   Bringing damage to.
5   *The being rightfully possessed ... aggravation of it*   Locke means here: Being the owner of great power and riches ... far from being an excuse for robbery and oppression, makes it much worse.
6   *by the law*   As a matter of law.

less he will, by actually putting himself into a state of war with his people, dissolve the government, and leave them to that defense which belongs to everyone in the state of nature: for of such things who can tell what the end will be? and a neighbor kingdom has shown the world an odd example. In all other cases the sacredness of the person exempts him from all inconveniencies, whereby he is secure, while the government stands, from all violence and harm whatsoever; than which there cannot be a wiser constitution: for the harm he can do in his own person not being likely to happen often, nor to extend itself far; nor being able by his single strength to subvert the laws, nor oppress the body of the people, should any prince have so much weakness, and ill nature as to be willing to do it, the inconveniency of some particular mischiefs, that may happen sometimes, when a heady prince comes to the throne, are well recompensed by the peace of the public, and security of the government, in the person of the chief magistrate, thus set out of the reach of danger: it being safer for the body, that some few private men should be sometimes in danger to suffer, than that the head of the republic should be easily, and upon slight occasions, exposed.

§ 206. Secondly, But this privilege, belonging only to the king's person, hinders not, but they may be questioned, opposed, and resisted, who use unjust force, though they pretend a commission from him, which the law authorizes not;[1] as is plain in the case of him that has the king's writ to arrest a man, which is a full commission from the king; and yet he that has it cannot break open a man's house to do it, nor execute this command of the king upon certain days, nor in certain places, though this commission have no such exception in it; but they are the limitations of the law, which if anyone transgress, the king's commission excuses him not: for the king's authority being given him only by the law, he cannot empower anyone to act against the law, or justify him, by his commission, in so doing; the commission, or command of any magistrate, where he has no authority, being as void and insignificant, as that of any private man; the difference between the one and the other, being that the magistrate has some authority so far, and to such ends, and the private man has none at all: for it is not the commission, but the authority, that gives the right of acting; and against the laws there can be no authority. But, notwithstanding such resistance, the king's person and authority are still both secured, and so no danger to governor or government.

---

1   *But this privilege ... authorizes not*   Locke means here: This privilege for the king's person does not extend to those who use unjust force, claiming to be commissioned by the king; they may be questioned, opposed, and resisted.

§ 207. Thirdly, Supposing a government wherein the person of the chief magistrate is not thus sacred; yet this doctrine of the lawfulness of resisting all unlawful exercises of his power, will not upon every slight occasion endanger him, or embroil the government: for where the injured party may be relieved, and his damages repaired by appeal to the law, there can be no pretence for force, which is only to be used where a man is intercepted from appealing to the law: for nothing is to be accounted[1] hostile force, but where it leaves not the remedy of such an appeal; and it is such force alone, that puts him that uses it into a state of war, and makes it lawful to resist him. A man with a sword in his hand demands my purse in the highway, when perhaps I have not twelve pence in my pocket: this man I may lawfully kill. To another I deliver 100 pounds to hold only while I alight, which he refuses to restore me, when I am got up again, but draws his sword to defend the possession of it by force, if I endeavor to retake it. The mischief this man does me is a hundred, or possibly a thousand times more than the other perhaps intended me (whom I killed before he really did me any); and yet I might lawfully kill the one, and cannot so much as hurt the other lawfully. The reason whereof is plain; because the one using force, which threatened my life, I could not have time to appeal to the law to secure it: and when it was gone, it was too late to appeal. The law could not restore life to my dead carcass: the loss was irreparable; which to prevent, the law of nature gave me a right to destroy him, who had put himself into a state of war with me, and threatened my destruction. But in the other case, my life not being in danger, I may have the benefit of appealing to the law, and have reparation for my 100 pounds that way.

§ 208. Fourthly, But if the unlawful acts done by the magistrate be maintained (by the power he has got), and the remedy which is due by law, be by the same power obstructed; yet the right of resisting, even in such manifest acts of tyranny, will not suddenly, or on slight occasions, disturb the government: for if it reach no farther than some private men's cases, though they have a right to defend themselves, and to recover by force what by unlawful force is taken from them; yet the right to do so will not easily engage them in a contest, wherein they are sure to perish; it being as impossible for one, or a few oppressed men to disturb the government, where the body of the people do not think themselves concerned in it, as for a raving madman, or heady[2] malcontent to overturn a well settled state; the people being as little apt to follow the one, as the other.

---

1   *accounted*   Counted as.
2   *heady*   Impetuous.

§ 209. But if either these illegal acts have extended to the majority of the people; or if the mischief and oppression has lighted only on some few, but in such cases, as the precedent, and consequences seem to threaten all; and they are persuaded in their consciences, that their laws, and with them their estates, liberties, and lives are in danger, and perhaps their religion too; how they will be hindered from resisting illegal force, used against them, I cannot tell. This is an inconvenience, I confess, that attends all governments whatsoever, when the governors have brought it to this pass, to be generally suspected of their people; the most dangerous state which they can possibly put themselves in. Wherein they are the less to be pitied, because it is so easy to be avoided; it being as impossible for a governor, if he really means the good of his people, and the preservation of them, and their laws together, not to make them see and feel it, as it is for the father of a family, not to let his children see he loves, and takes care of them.

§ 210. But if all the world shall observe pretences of one kind, and actions of another; arts used to elude the law, and the trust of prerog ative (which is an arbitrary power in some things left in the prince's hand to do good, not harm to the people) employed contrary to the end for which it was given: if the people shall find the ministers and subordinate magistrates chosen suitable to such ends, and favored, or laid by, proportionably as[1] they promote or oppose them: if they see several experiments made of arbitrary power, and that religion underhand[2] favored, (though publicly proclaimed against) which is readiest to introduce it; and the operators[3] in it supported, as much as may be; and when that cannot be done, yet approved still, and liked the better: if a long train of actions show the councils all tending that way; how can a man any more hinder himself from being persuaded in his own mind, which way things are going; or from casting about how to save himself, than he could from believing the captain of the ship he was in, was carrying him, and the rest of the company, to Algiers,[4] when he found him always steering that course, though cross winds, leaks in his ship, and want of men and provisions did often force him to turn his course another way for some time, which he steadily returned to again, as soon as the wind, weather, and other circumstances would let him?

---

1 *laid by, proportionably as* Dismissed, depending on whether they promote or oppose them.
2 *underhand* Secretly.
3 *operators* Officials (of the religion).
4 *Algiers* The capital of Algeria, in North Africa. A particularly nasty—pirate-ridden—place in Locke's day.

Chapter 19. Of the Dissolution of Government

§ 211. He that will with any clearness speak of the dissolution of government, ought in the first place to distinguish between the dissolution of the society and the dissolution of the government. That which makes the community, and brings men out of the loose state of nature, into one politic society, is the agreement which everyone has with the rest to incorporate, and act as one body, and so be one distinct commonwealth. The usual, and almost only way whereby this union is dissolved, is the inroad of foreign force making a conquest upon them: for in that case, (not being able to maintain and support themselves, as one entire and independent body) the union belonging to that body which consisted therein, must necessarily cease, and so everyone return to the state he was in before, with a liberty to shift for himself, and provide for his own safety, as he thinks fit, in some other society. Whenever the society is dissolved, it is certain the government of that society cannot remain. Thus conquerors' swords often cut up governments by[1] the roots, and mangle societies to pieces, separating the subdued or scattered multitude from the protection of, and dependence on, that society which ought to have preserved them from violence. The world is too well instructed in, and too forward[2] to allow of, this way of dissolving of governments, to need any more to be said of it; and there wants not much argument to prove, that where the society is dissolved, the government cannot remain; that being as impossible, as for the frame of an house to subsist when the materials of it are scattered and dissipated by a whirlwind, or jumbled into a confused heap by an earthquake.

§ 212. Besides this overturning from without, governments are dissolved from within,

First, When the legislative is altered. Civil society being a state of peace, among those who are of it, from whom the state of war is excluded by the umpirage,[3] which they have provided in their legislative, for the ending all differences that may arise among any of them, it is in their legislative, that the members of a commonwealth are united, and combined together into one coherent living body. This is the soul that gives form, life, and unity, to the commonwealth: from hence the several members have their mutual influence, sympathy, and connection: and therefore, when the legislative is broken, or dissolved, dissolution and death follows: for the essence and union of the society consisting in having one will, the legislative, when once established by the ma-

---

1 *cut up governments by*   Cut off governments at.
2 *forward*   Ready.
3 *the umpirage*   The existence of an arbitrator or arbitration process.

jority, has the declaring, and as it were keeping of that will. The constitution of the legislative is the first and fundamental act of society, whereby provision is made for the continuation of their union, under the direction of persons, and bonds of laws, made by persons authorized thereunto, by the consent and appointment of the people, without which no one man, or number of men, among them, can have authority of making laws that shall be binding to the rest. When any one, or more, shall take upon them to make laws, whom the people have not appointed so to do, they make laws without authority, which the people are not therefore bound to obey; by which means they come again to be out of subjection, and may constitute to themselves a new legislative, as they think best, being in full liberty to resist the force of those, who without authority would impose any thing upon them. Everyone is at the disposure of his own will,[1] when those who had, by the delegation of the society, the declaring of the public will, are excluded from it, and others usurp the place, who have no such authority or delegation.

§ 213. This being usually brought about by such in the common wealth who misuse the power they have; it is hard to consider it aright, and know at whose door to lay it,[2] without knowing the form of government in which it happens. Let us suppose then the legislative placed in the concurrence[3] of three distinct persons.

1. A single hereditary person, having the constant, supreme, executive power, and with it the power of convoking and dissolving the other two within certain periods of time.

2. An assembly of hereditary nobility.

3. An assembly of representatives chosen, pro tempore,[4] by the people. Such a form of government supposed,[5] it is evident,

§ 214. First, That when such a single person, or prince, sets up his own arbitrary will in place of the laws, which are the will of the society, declared by the legislative, then the legislative is changed: for that being in effect the legislative, whose rules and laws are put in execution, and required to be obeyed; when other laws are set up, and other rules pretended, and enforced, than what the legislative, constituted by the society, have enacted, it is plain that the legislative is changed.[6]

---

1 *at the disposure of his own will* Free to do what he wants.

2 *at whose door to lay it* Whom to blame it on.

3 *concurrence* Cooperation.

4 *pro tempore* Latin: for a limited period.

5 *supposed* Assumed.

6 *for that being in effect ... legislative is changed* This means: What constitutes a legislature is applying rules and laws, and requiring them to be obeyed; so when laws are set up and rules announced and enforced other than those enacted by the legislature set up by the society, clearly a new legislature is in place.

Whoever introduces new laws, not being thereunto authorized by the fundamental appointment of the society, or subverts the old, disowns and overturns the power by which they were made, and so sets up a new legislative.

§ 215. Secondly, When the prince hinders the legislative from assembling in its due time, or from acting freely, pursuant to those ends for which it was constituted, the legislative is altered: for it is not a certain number of men, no, nor their meeting, unless they have also freedom of debating, and leisure of perfecting, what is for the good of the society, wherein the legislative consists: when these are taken away or altered, so as to deprive the society of the due exercise of their power, the legislative is truly altered; for it is not names that constitute governments, but the use and exercise of those powers that were intended to accompany them; so that he, who takes away the freedom, or hinders the acting of the legislative in its due seasons, in effect takes away the legislative, and puts an end to the government.

§ 216. Thirdly, When, by the arbitrary power of the prince, the electors,[1] or ways of election, are altered, without the consent, and contrary to the common interest of the people, there also the legislative is altered: for, if others than those whom the society has authorized thereunto, do choose, or in another way than what the society has prescribed, those chosen are not the legislative appointed by the people.

§ 217. Fourthly, The delivery also of the people into the subjection of a foreign power, either by the prince, or by the legislative, is certainly a change of the legislative, and so a dissolution of the government: for the end why people entered into society being to be preserved one entire, free, independent society, to be governed by its own laws; this is lost, whenever they are given up into the power of another.

§ 218. Why, in such a constitution as this, the dissolution of the government in these cases is to be imputed to[2] the prince, is evident; because he, having the force, treasure[3] and offices of the state to employ, and often persuading himself, or being flattered by others, that as supreme magistrate he is incapable of control;[4] he alone is in a condition to make great advances toward such changes, under pretence of lawful authority, and has it in his hands to terrify or suppress opposers, as factious,[5] seditious, and enemies to the government: whereas no

---

1   *electors*   People who are to vote.
2   *imputed to*   Blamed on.
3   *treasure*   Treasury.
4   *incapable of control*   Can't be told what to do.
5   *factious*   Promoting internal dissension.

other part of the legislative, or people, is capable by themselves to attempt any alteration of the legislative, without open and visible rebellion, apt enough to be taken notice of, which, when it prevails, produces effects very little different from foreign conquest. Besides, the prince in such a form of government, having the power of dissolving the other parts of the legislative, and thereby rendering them private persons, they can never in opposition to him, or without his concurrence, alter the legislative by a law, his consent being necessary to give any of their decrees that sanction. But yet so far as the other parts of the legislative any way contribute to any attempt upon the government, and do either promote, or not, what lies in them,[1] hinder such designs, they are guilty, and partake in this, which is certainly the greatest crime men can be guilty of one towards another.

§ 219. There is one way more whereby such a government may be dissolved, and that is: When he who has the supreme executive power, neglects and abandons that charge, so that the laws already made can no longer be put in execution. This is demonstratively[2] to reduce all to anarchy, and so effectually to dissolve the government: for laws not being made for themselves, but to be, by their execution, the bonds of the society, to keep every part of the body politic in its due place and function; when that totally ceases, the government visibly ceases, and the people become a confused multitude, without order or connection. Where there is no longer the administration of justice, for the securing of men's rights, nor any remaining power within the community to direct the force, or provide for the necessities of the public, there certainly is no government left. Where the laws cannot be executed, it is all one as if there were no laws; and a government without laws is, I suppose, a mystery in politics, unconceivable to human capacity, and inconsistent with human society.

§ 220. In these and the like cases, when the government is dissolved, the people are at liberty to provide for themselves, by erecting a new legislative, differing from the other, by the change of persons, or form, or both, as they shall find it most for their safety and good: for the society can never, by the fault of another, lose the native and original right it has to preserve itself, which can only be done by a settled legislative, and a fair and impartial execution of the laws made by it. But the state of mankind is not so miserable that they are not capable of using this remedy, till it be too late to look for any. To tell people they may provide for themselves, by erecting a new legislative, when by oppression, artifice, or being delivered over to a foreign power,

---

1 *what lies in them* When they could have done so.
2 *demonstratively* Manifestly.

their old one is gone, is only to tell them, they may expect relief when it is too late, and the evil is past cure. This is in effect no more than to bid them first be slaves, and then to take care of their liberty; and when their chains are on, tell them, they may act like freemen. This, if barely so, is rather mockery than relief; and men can never be secure from tyranny, if there be no means to escape it till they are perfectly under it: and therefore it is, that they have not only a right to get out of it, but to prevent it.

§ 221. There is therefore, secondly, another way whereby governments are dissolved, and that is, when the legislative, or the prince, either of them, act contrary to their trust. First, The legislative acts against the trust reposed in them, when they endeavor to invade the property of the subject, and to make themselves, or any part of the community, masters, or arbitrary disposers of the lives, liberties, or fortunes of the people.

§ 222. The reason why men enter into society, is the preservation of their property; and the end why they choose and authorize a legislative, is, that there may be laws made, and rules set, as guards and fences to the properties of all the members of the society, to limit the power, and moderate the dominion, of every part and member of the society: for since it can never be supposed to be the will of the society, that the legislative should have a power to destroy that which everyone designs to secure, by entering into society, and for which the people submitted themselves to legislators of their own making; whenever the legislators endeavor to take away, and destroy the property of the people, or to reduce them to slavery under arbitrary power, they put themselves into a state of war with the people, who are thereupon absolved from any farther obedience, and are left to the common refuge, which God has provided for all men, against force and violence. Whenever therefore the legislative shall transgress this fundamental rule of society; and either by ambition, fear, folly or corruption, endeavor to grasp themselves, or put into the hands of any other, an absolute power over the lives, liberties, and estates of the people; by this breach of trust they forfeit the power the people had put into their hands for quite contrary ends, and it devolves to the people, who have a right to resume their original liberty, and, by the establishment of a new legislative, (such as they shall think fit) provide for their own safety and security, which is the end for which they are in society. What I have said here, concerning the legislative in general, holds true also concerning the supreme executor, who having a double trust put in him, both to have a part in the legislative, and the supreme execution of the law, acts against both, when he goes about to set up his own arbitrary will as the law of the society. He acts also contrary to his trust, when he either employs the force, treasure, and offices of the society, to corrupt the representatives, and gain them to his purposes; or openly preengages[1] the electors, and prescribes to their choice, such, whom he has, by solicitations, threats, promises, or otherwise, won to his designs; and employs them to bring in such,[2] who have promised beforehand what to vote, and what to enact. Thus to regulate candidates and electors, and new-model[3] the ways of election, what is it but to cut up the government by the roots, and poison the very fountain of public security? for the people having reserved to themselves the choice of their representatives, as the fence to their properties, could do it for no other end, but that they might always be freely chosen, and so chosen, freely act, and advise, as the necessity of the commonwealth, and the public good should, upon examination, and mature debate, be judged to require. This, those who give their votes before they hear the debate, and have weighed the reasons on all sides, are not capable of doing. To prepare such an assembly as this, and endeavor to set up the declared abettors of his own will, for the true representatives of the people, and the law-makers of the society, is certainly as great a breach of trust, and as perfect a declaration of a design to subvert the government, as is possible to be met with. To which, if one shall add rewards and punishments visibly employed to the same end, and all the arts of perverted law made use of, to take off and destroy all that stand in the way of such a design, and will not comply and consent to betray the liberties of their country, it will be past doubt what is doing. What power they ought to have in the society, who thus employ it contrary to the trust went along with it in its first institution, is easy to determine; and one cannot but see, that he, who has once attempted any such thing as this, cannot any longer be trusted.

§ 223. To this perhaps it will be said,[4] that the people being ignorant, and always discontented, to lay the foundation of government in the unsteady opinion and uncertain humor of the people, is to expose it to certain ruin; and no government will be able long to subsist, if the people may set up a new legislative, whenever they take offence at the old one. To this I answer, Quite the contrary. People are not so easily got out of their old forms, as some are apt to suggest. They are hardly to be prevailed with to amend the acknowledged faults in the frame they have been accustomed to. And if there be any original defects, or adventitious[5] ones introduced by time, or corruption; it is not an easy

---

1 *preengages*   Wins over or binds beforehand.
2 *bring in such*   Elect those.
3 *new-model*   Reshape.
4 *it will be said*   It will be objected.
5 *adventitious*   Added from outside, accidental.

thing to get them changed, even when all the world sees there is an opportunity for it. This slowness and aversion in the people to quit their old constitutions, has, in the many revolutions which have been seen in this kingdom, in this and former ages, still kept us to, or, after some interval of fruitless attempts, still brought us back again to our old legislative of king, lords and commons: and whatever provocations have made the crown be taken from some of our princes' heads, they never carried the people so far as to place it in another line.[1]

§ 224. But it will be said, this hypothesis lays[2] a ferment for frequent rebellion. To which I answer,

First, No more than any other hypothesis: for when the people are made miserable, and find themselves exposed to the ill usage of arbitrary power, cry up their governors, as much as you will, for sons of Jupiter;[3] let them be sacred and divine, descended, or authorized from heaven; give them out for whom or what you please, the same will happen. The people generally ill treated, and contrary to right, will be ready upon any occasion to ease themselves of a burden that sits heavy upon them. They will wish, and seek for the opportunity, which in the change, weakness and accidents of human affairs, seldom delays long to offer itself. He must have lived but a little while in the world, who has not seen examples of this in his time; and he must have read very little, who cannot produce examples of it in all sorts of governments in the world.

§ 225. Secondly, I answer, such revolutions happen not upon every little mismanagement in public affairs. Great mistakes in the ruling part, many wrong and inconvenient laws, and all the slips of human frailty, will be born by the people without mutiny or murmur. But if a long train of abuses, prevarications[4] and artifices, all tending the same way, make the design visible to the people, and they cannot but feel what they lie under, and see whither they are going; it is not to be wondered, that they should then rouse themselves, and endeavor to put the rule into such hands which may secure to them the ends for which government was at first erected; and without which, ancient names, and specious forms,[5] are so far from being better, that they are much worse, than the state of nature, or pure anarchy; the inconveniencies being all as great and as near, but the remedy farther off and more difficult.

---

1 *line* Line of descent.
2 *lays* Creates.
3 *for sons of Jupiter* As if they were sons of Jupiter (who was the patron deity of the ancient Roman state, the god of laws and social order).
4 *prevarications* Avoidances of telling the truth.
5 *specious forms* Deceptively attractive rituals.

§ 226. Thirdly, I answer, that this doctrine of a power in the people of providing for their safety anew, by a new legislative, when their legislators have acted contrary to their trust, by invading their property, is the best fence against rebellion, and the probablest[1] means to hinder it: for rebellion being an opposition, not to persons, but authority, which is founded only in the constitutions and laws of the government; those, whoever they be, who by force break through, and by force justify their violation of them, are truly and properly rebels: for when men, by entering into society and civil-government, have excluded force, and introduced laws for the preservation of property, peace, and unity among themselves, those who set up force again in opposition to the laws, do rebellare,[2] that is, bring back again the state of war, and are properly rebels: which they who are in power, (by the pretence they have to authority, the temptation of force they have in their hands, and the flattery of those about them) being likeliest to do; the most proper way to prevent the evil, is to show them the danger and injustice of it, who are under the greatest temptation to run into it.

§ 227. In both the aforementioned cases, when either the legislative is changed, or the legislators act contrary to the end for which they were constituted; those who are guilty are guilty of rebellion: for if anyone by force takes away the established legislative of any society, and the laws by them made, pursuant to their trust, he thereby takes away the umpirage, which everyone had consented to, for a peaceable decision of all their controversies, and a bar to the state of war among them. They, who remove, or change the legislative, take away this decisive power, which nobody can have, but by the appointment and consent of the people; and so destroying the authority which the people did, and nobody else can set up, and introducing a power which the people has not authorized, they actually introduce a state of war, which is that of force without authority: and thus, by removing the legislative established by the society, (in whose decisions the people acquiesced and united, as to that of their own will) they untie the knot, and expose the people a-new to the state of war. And if those, who by force take away the legislative, are rebels, the legislators themselves, as has been shown, can be no less esteemed so; when they, who were set up for the protection, and preservation of the people, their liberties and properties, shall by force invade and endeavor to take them away; and so they putting themselves into a state of war with those who made them

---

1 *probablest* Most likely.

2 *rebellare* Latin: rebel. This word derives from *bellare*, to make war; so adding the initial *re* (= again) suggests making war again. That may be why Locke uses the Latin word: for him, to rebel and destroy the government is to re-institute a state of war.

the protectors and guardians of their peace, are properly, and with the greatest aggravation, rebellantes,[1] rebels.

§ 228. But if they, who say it lays a foundation for rebellion, mean that it may occasion civil wars, or intestine broils,[2] to tell the people they are absolved from[3] obedience when illegal attempts are made upon their liberties or properties, and may oppose the unlawful violence of those who were their magistrates, when they invade their properties contrary to the trust put in them; and that therefore this doctrine is not to be allowed, being so destructive to the peace of the world: they may as well say, upon the same ground, that honest men may not oppose robbers or pirates, because this may occasion disorder or bloodshed. If any mischief come in such cases, it is not to be charged upon him who defends his own right, but on him that invades his neighbors. If the innocent honest man must quietly quit all he has, for peace sake, to him who will lay violent hands upon it, I desire it may be considered, what a kind of peace there will be in the world, which consists only in violence and rapine; and which is to be maintained only for the benefit of robbers and oppressors. Who would not think it an admirable peace betwixt the mighty and the mean, when the lamb, without resistance, yielded his throat to be torn by the imperious wolf? Polyphemus's den[4] gives us a perfect pattern of such a peace, and such a government, wherein Ulysses and his companions had nothing to do, but quietly to suffer themselves to be devoured. And no doubt Ulysses, who was a prudent man, preached up passive obedience, and exhorted them to a quiet submission, by representing to them of what concernment peace was to mankind; and by showing the inconveniencies might happen, if they should offer to resist Polyphemus, who had now the power over them.

§ 229. The end of government is the good of mankind; and which is best for mankind, that the people should be always exposed to the boundless will of tyranny, or that the rulers should be sometimes liable to be opposed, when they grow exorbitant in the use of their power, and employ it for the destruction, and not the preservation of the properties of their people?

§ 230. Nor[5] let anyone say, that mischief can arise from hence, as often as it shall please a busy head, or turbulent spirit, to desire the al-

---

1   *rebellantes*   Latin: rebels; but see previous note.
2   *intestine broils*   Internal unrest.
3   *absolved from*   Relieved of the obligation of.
4   *Polyphemus's den*   In Homer's *Odyssey*, Polyphemus is a ferocious and horrible one-eyed giant (a Cyclops) who traps Ulysses and his men in his cave and begins eating them. Contrary to Locke's sarcastic suggestion, Ulysses hatches an ingenious scheme to blind Polyphemus and escape.
5   *Nor*   Do not.

teration of the government. It is true, such men may stir, whenever they please; but it will be only to their own just ruin and perdition: for till the mischief be grown general, and the ill designs of the rulers become visible, or their attempts sensible to the greater part,[1] the people, who are more disposed to suffer than right themselves by resistance, are not apt to stir. The examples of particular injustice, or oppression of here and there an unfortunate man, moves them not. But if they universally have a persuasion, grounded upon manifest evidence, that designs are carrying on[2] against their liberties, and the general course and tendency of things cannot but give them strong suspicions of the evil intention of their governors, who is to be blamed for it? Who can help it, if they, who might avoid it, bring themselves into this suspicion? Are the people to be blamed, if they have the sense of rational creatures, and can think of things no otherwise than as they find and feel them? And is it not rather their fault, who put things into such a posture, that they would not have them thought to be as they are? I grant, that the pride, ambition, and turbulency of private men have sometimes caused great disorders in commonwealths, and factions have been fatal to states and kingdoms. But whether the mischief has oftener begun in the people's wantonness,[3] and a desire to cast off the lawful authority of their rulers, or in the rulers insolence, and endeavors to get and exercise an arbitrary power over their people; whether oppression, or disobedience, gave the first rise to the disorder, I leave it to impartial history to determine. This I am sure, whoever, either ruler or subject, by force goes about to invade the rights of either prince or people, and lays the foundation for overturning the constitution and frame of any just government, is highly guilty of the greatest crime, I think, a man is capable of, being to answer for all those mischiefs of blood, rapine, and desolation, which the breaking to pieces of governments bring on a country. And he who does it, is justly to be esteemed the common enemy and pest of mankind, and is to be treated accordingly.

§ 231. That subjects or foreigners, attempting by force on the properties of any people, may be resisted with force, is agreed on all hands. But that magistrates, doing the same thing, may be resisted, has of late been denied: as if those who had the greatest privileges and advantages by the law, had thereby a power to break those laws, by which alone they were set in a better place than their brethren: whereas their offence is thereby the greater, both as being ungrateful for the greater

---

1   *sensible to the greater part*   Visible, or obvious, to the majority (of people).
2   *designs are carrying on*   Plots are being carried out.
3   *wantonness*   Unruliness, irresponsibility.

share they have by the law, and breaking also that trust, which is put into their hands by their brethren.

§ 232. Whosoever uses force without right, as everyone does in society, who does it without law, puts himself into a state of war with those against whom he so uses it; and in that state all former ties are cancelled, all other rights cease, and everyone has a right to defend himself, and to resist the aggressor. This is so evident, that Barclay[1] himself, that great assertor of the power and sacredness of kings, is forced to confess, that it is lawful for the people, in some cases, to resist their king; and that too in a chapter, wherein he pretends to show, that the divine law shuts up[2] the people from all manner of rebellion. Whereby it is evident, even by his own doctrine, that, since they may in some cases resist, all resisting of princes is not rebellion.

His words are these:[3]

Quod siquis dicat, Ergone populus tyrannicae crudelitati et furori jugulum semper praebebit? Ergone multitudo civitates suas fame, ferro, et flamma vastari, seque, conjuges, et liberos fortunae ludibrio et tyranni libidini exponi, inque omnia vitae pericula omnesque miserias et molestias a rege deduci patientur? Num illis quod omni animantium generi est a natura tributum, denegari debet, ut sc. vim vi repellant, seseque ab injuria tueantur? Huic breviter responsum sit, populo universo negari defensionem, quae juris naturalis est, neque ultionem quae praeter naturam est adversus regem concedi debere. Quapropter si rex non in singulares tantum personas aliquot privatum odium exerceat, sed corpus etiam reipublicae, cujus ipse, caput est—i.e., totum populum, vel insignem aliquam ejus partem immani et intoleranda saevitia seu tyrannide divexet; populo, quidem hoc casu resistendi ac tuendi se ab injuria potestas competit, sed tuendi se tantum, non enim in principem invadendi: et restituendae injuriae illatae, non recedendi a debita reverentia propter acceptum injuriam. Praesentem denique impetum propulsandi non vim praeteritam ulciscendi jus habet. Horum enim alterum a natura est, ut vitani scilicet corpusque tueamur. Alterum vero contra naturam, ut inferior de superiori supplicium sumat. Quod itaque populus malum, antequam factum sit, impedire potest, ne

---

1　*Barclay*　William Barclay (c. 1546-1608), obscure Scottish jurist and political theorist.
2　*shuts up*　Blocks.
3　*His words are these*　See below for Locke's English translation. (This is one of a series of Latin quotations that Locke translates.)

fiat, id postquam factum est, in regem authorem sceleris vindi-
care non potest, populus igitur hoc amplius quam privatus
quispiam habet: Quod huic, vel ipsis adversariis judicibus, ex-
cepto Buchanano, nullum nisi in patientia remedium superest.
Cum ille si intolerabilis tyrannis est (modicum enim ferre
omnino debet) resistere cum reverentia possit.—Barclay, *Contra Monarchomachos*, I. iii. c. 8.

In English thus:

§ 233. But if anyone should ask, Must the people then always lay
themselves open to the cruelty and rage of tyranny? Must they
see their cities pillaged, and laid in ashes, their wives and children
exposed to the tyrant's lust and fury, and themselves and families
reduced by their king to ruin, and all the miseries of want and
oppression, and yet sit still? Must men alone be debarred the
common privilege of opposing force with force, which nature allows so freely to all other creatures for their preservation from injury? I answer: Self-defense is a part of the law of nature; nor
can it be denied the community, even against the king himself:
but to revenge themselves upon him, must by no means be allowed them; it being not agreeable to[1] that law. Wherefore if the
king shall show an hatred, not only to some particular persons,
but sets himself against the body of the commonwealth, whereof
he is the head, and shall, with intolerable ill usage, cruelly tyr-
annize over the whole, or a considerable part of the people, in
this case the people have a right to resist and defend themselves
from injury: but it must be with this caution, that they only defend
themselves, but do not attack their prince: they may repair the
damages received, but must not for any provocation exceed the
bounds of due reverence and respect. They may repulse the present attempt, but must not revenge past violences: for it is natural
for us to defend life and limb, but that an inferior should punish
a superior, is against nature. The mischief which is designed
them, the people may prevent before it be done; but when it is
done, they must not revenge it on the king, though author of the
villainy. This therefore is the privilege of the people in general,
above what any private person has; that particular men are allowed by our adversaries themselves (Buchanan[2] only excepted)

---

1   *agreeable to*   In conformity with.
2   *Buchanan*   George Buchanan (1506-82), Scottish poet and political writer who
    argued that the monarch's power came from the people, not from divine right.

to have no other remedy but patience; but the body of the people may with respect resist intolerable tyranny; for when it is but moderate, they ought to endure it.

§ 234. Thus far that great advocate of monarchical power allows of resistance.

§ 235. It is true, he has annexed two limitations to it, to no purpose: First, He says, it must be with reverence.

Secondly, It must be without retribution, or punishment; and the reason he gives is, because an inferior cannot punish a superior.

First, How to resist force without striking again, or how to strike with reverence, will need some skill to make intelligible. He that shall oppose an assault only with a shield to receive the blows, or in any more respectful posture, without a sword in his hand, to abate the confidence and force of the assailant, will quickly be at an end of his resistance, and will find such a defense serve only to draw on himself the worse usage. This is as ridiculous a way of resisting, as Juvenal thought it of fighting; ubi tu pulsas, ego vapulo tantum.[1] And the success of the combat will be unavoidably the same he there describes it:

Libertas pauperis haec est:
Pulsatus rogat, & pugnis concisus, àdorat,
Ut liceat paucis cum dentibus inde reverti.[2]

This will always be the event of such an imaginary resistance, where men may not strike again. He therefore who may resist, must be allowed to strike. And then let our author, or anybody else, join a knock on the head, or a cut on the face, with as much reverence and respect as he thinks fit. He that can reconcile blows and reverence, may, for aught I know, desire for his pains, a civil, respectful cudgeling wherever he can meet with it.

Secondly, As to his second, An inferior cannot punish a superior; that is true, generally speaking, while he is his superior. But to resist force with force, being the state of war that levels the parties, cancels all former relation of reverence, respect, and superiority: and then the odds that remains, is, that he, who opposes the unjust aggressor, has

---

1 *ubi tu ... tantum*   Latin: when you do all the thrashing and I get all the blows. This and the following quotation are from Juvenal, Roman satirist (60?-140? CE). In his *Third Satire*, this quote appears at line 289, and the following at lines 299-301.

2 *Libertas pauperis ... inde reverti*   Latin: such is the liberty of the poor man: having been pounded and cuffed into a jelly, he begs and prays to be allowed to return home with a few teeth in his head.

this superiority over him, that he has a right, when he prevails, to punish the offender, both for the breach of the peace, and all the evils that
followed upon it. Barclay therefore, in another place, more coherently
to himself,[1] denies it to be lawful to resist a king in any case. But he
there assigns two cases, whereby a king may un-king himself. His
words are,

Quid ergo, nulline casus incidere possunt quibus populo sese
erigere atque in regem impotentius dominantem arma capere et
invadere jure suo suaque authoritate liceat? Nulli certe quamdiu
rex manet. Semper enim ex divinis id obstat, Regem honorifi-
cato, et qui potestati resistit, Dei ordinationi resistit; non alias
igitur in eum populo potestas est quam si id committat propter
quod ipso jure rex esse desinat. Tunc enim se ipse principatu
exuit atque in privatis constituit liber; hoc modo populus et superior efficitur, reverso ad eum scilicet jure illo quod ante regem
inauguratum in interregno habuit. At sunt paucorum generum
commissa ejusmodi quae hunc effectum pariunt. At ego cum
plurima animo perlustrem, duo tantum invenio, duos, inquam,
casus quibus rex ipso facto ex rege non regem se facit et omni
honore et dignitate regali atque in subditos potestate destituit;
quorum etiam meminit Winzerus. Horum unus est, si regnum
disperdat, quemadmodum de Nerone fertur, quod is nempe sen-
atum populumque Romanum atque adeo urbem ipsam ferro
flammaque vastare, ac novas sibi sedes quaerere decrevisset. Et
de Caligula, quod palam denunciarit se neque civem neque
principem senatui amplius fore, inque animo habuerit, in-
terempto utriusque ordinis electissimo, quoque Alexandriam
commigrare, ac ut populum uno ictu interimeret, unam ei cer-
vicem optavit. Talia cum rex aliquis meditatur et molitur serio,
omnem regnandi curam et animum ilico abjicit, ac proinde imperium in subditos amittit, ut dominus servi pro derelicto habiti,
dominium.

§ 236. Alter casus est, si rex in alicujus clientelam se contulit,
ac regnum quod liberum a majoribus et populo traditum accepit,
alienae ditioni mancipavit. Nam tunc quamvis forte non ea
mente id agit populo plane ut incommodet; tamen quia quod
praecipuum est regiae dignitatis amisit, ut summus scilicet in
regno secundum Deum sit, et solo Deo inferior, atque populum
etiam totum ignorantem vel invitum, cujus libertatem sartam et
tectam conservare debuit, in alterius gentis ditionem et potes-

---

1 *coherently to himself* Consistently.

tatem dedidit; hac velut quadam rengi abalienatione effecit, ut
nec quod ipse in regno imperium habuit retineat, nec in eum cui
collatum voluit, juris quicquam transferat, atque ita eo facto
liberum jam et suae potestatis populum relinquit, cujus rei ex-
emplum unum annales Scotici suppeditant.—Barclay, *Contra
Monarchomachos*, I. iii., c. 16.

Which in English runs thus:

§ 237. What then, can there no case happen wherein the people
may of right, and by their own authority, help themselves, take
arms, and set upon their king, imperiously domineering over
them? None at all, while he remains a king. "Honor the king,"
and "He that resists the power, resists the ordinance of God,"
are divine oracles[1] that will never permit it. The people therefore
can never come by a power over him, unless he does something
that makes him cease to be a king: for then he divests himself of
his crown and dignity, and returns to the state of a private man,
and the people become free and superior, the power which they
had in the interregnum,[2] before they crowned him king, devolv-
ing to them again. But there are but few miscarriages which
bring the matter to this state. After considering it well on all
sides, I can find but two. Two cases there are, I say, whereby a
king, ipso facto,[3] becomes no king, and loses all power and regal
authority over his people; which are also taken notice of by
Winzerus.[4]

   The first is, If he endeavor to overturn the government, that is,
if he have a purpose and design to ruin the kingdom and commonwealth, as it is recorded of Nero,[5] that he resolved to cut off
the senate and people of Rome, lay the city waste with fire and
sword, and then remove to some other place. And of Caligula,[6]

---

1   *oracles*   Revelations.
2   *interregnum*   Latin: time between one reign and the next.
3   *ipso facto*   Latin: as a result of that fact in particular.
4   *Winzerus*   Ninian Winzet (c. 1518-92), Scottish Benedictine Abbot, author of
    pamphlets replying to Barclay, defending the power of the (constitutional)
    monarch.
5   *Nero*   Nero Claudius Caesar (37-68), emperor of Rome, with a very bad reputa-
    tion: thought to have murdered his mother, wife, and mistress, to have set fire to
    Rome, etc.
6   *Caligula*   Gaius Julius Caesar Germanicus (12-41), Roman emperor with a rep-
    utation for madness and misrule.

that he openly declared, that he would be no longer a head to the people or senate, and that he had it in his thoughts to cut off the worthiest men of both ranks, and then retire to Alexandria: and he wished that the people had but one neck, that he might dispatch them all at a blow. Such designs as these, when any king harbors in his thoughts, and seriously promotes, he immediately gives up all care and thought of the commonwealth; and consequently forfeits the power of governing his subjects, as a master does the dominion over his slaves whom he has abandoned.

§ 238. The other case is, When a king makes himself the dependent of another, and subjects his kingdom which his ancestors left him, and the people put free into his hands, to the dominion of another: for however perhaps it may not be his intention to prejudice the people; yet because he has hereby lost the principal part of legal dignity, viz. to be next and immediately under God, supreme in his kingdom; and also because he betrayed or forced his people, whose liberty he ought to have carefully preserved, into the power and dominion of a foreign nation. By this, as it were, alienation of his kingdom, he himself loses the power he had in it before, without transferring any the least right to those on whom he would have bestowed it; and so by this act sets the people free, and leaves them at their own disposal. One example of this is to be found in the *Scotch Annals*.

§ 239. In these cases Barclay, the great champion of absolute monarchy, is forced to allow, that a king may be resisted, and ceases to be a king. That is, in short, not to multiply cases, in whatsoever he has no authority, there he is no king, and may be resisted: for wherever the authority ceases, the king ceases too, and becomes like other men who have no authority. And these two cases he instances in, differ little from those above mentioned, to be destructive to governments, only that he has omitted the principle from which his doctrine flows: and that is, the breach of trust, in not preserving the form of government agreed on, and in not intending the end of government itself, which is the public good and preservation of property. When a king has dethroned himself, and put himself in a state of war with his people, what shall hinder them from prosecuting him who is no king, as they would any other man, who has put himself into a state of war with them, Barclay, and those of his opinion, would do well to tell us. This farther I desire may be taken notice of out of Barclay, that he says, "The mischief that is designed them, the people may prevent before it be done," whereby he allows resistance when tyranny is but in design. "Such designs as these," says he, "when any king harbors in his thoughts and seriously promotes, he immediately gives up all care and thought of the commonwealth," so that, according to him, the neglect of the public good is to be taken as an evidence of such design, or at least for a sufficient cause of resistance. And the reason of all, he gives in these words: "Because he betrayed or forced his people, whose liberty he ought carefully to have preserved." What he adds, "into the power and dominion of a foreign nation," signifies nothing, the fault and forfeiture[1] lying in the loss of their liberty, which he ought to have preserved, and not in any distinction of the persons to whose dominion they were subjected. The people's right is equally invaded, and their liberty lost, whether they are made slaves to any of their own, or a foreign nation; and in this lies the injury, and against this only have they the right of defense. And there are instances to be found in all countries, which show, that it is not the change of nations in the persons of their governors, but the change of government, that gives the offence. Bilson,[2] a bishop of our church, and a great stickler for the power and prerogative of princes, does, if I mistake not, in his treatise of Christian subjection, acknowledge, that princes may forfeit their power, and their title to the obedience of their subjects; and if there needed authority in a case where reason is so plain, I could send my reader to Bracton, Fortescue, and the author of the Mirrour,[3] and others, writers that cannot be suspected to be ignorant of our government, or enemies to it. But I thought Hooker alone might be enough to satisfy those men, who relying on him for their ecclesiastical polity,[4] are by a strange fate carried to deny those principles upon which he builds it. Whether they are herein made the tools of more cunning workmen, to pull down their own fabric, they were best look.[5] This I am sure, their civil pol-

---

1 *forfeiture* Transgression, crime.

2 *Bilson* Thomas Bilson (c. 1546-1616), author of *The True Difference between Christian Subjection and Unnatural Rebellion* (1586), which argued that, despite the fact that subjects must submit to royal authority in general, in certain cases revolt against this authority is justified.

3 *Bracton, Fortescue, and the author of the Mirrour* Henry de Bracton (d. 1268), English lawyer, argued in *De legibus et consuietudinibus Angliae* (1569) that the king is supreme ruler in his realm, but subject to law; Sir John Fortescue (1394-1476) wrote several books defending the idea that laws required consent of both king and people; the editor and principal contributor to *The Mirror for Magistrates* (1559) was William Baldwin; it is a collection of poems about the downfall of historical rulers, intended to warn against abuse of power.

4 *ecclesiastical polity* Principles of governance of the church.

5 *they were best look* They had better watch out.

icy is so new, so dangerous, and so destructive to both rulers and people, that as former ages never could bear the broaching[1] of it; so it may be hoped, those to come, redeemed[2] from the impositions of these Egyptian under-task-masters,[3] will abhor the memory of such servile flatterers, who, while it seemed to serve their turn, resolved[4] all government into absolute tyranny, and would have all men born to, what their mean souls fitted them for, slavery.

§ 240. Here, it is like,[5] the common question will be made,[6] "Who shall be judge, whether the prince or legislative act contrary to their trust?" This, perhaps, ill-affected and factious men may spread among the people, when the prince only makes use of his due prerogative. To this I reply, The people shall be judge; for who shall be judge whether his trustee or deputy acts well, and according to the trust reposed in him, but he who deputes him, and must, by having deputed him, have still a power to discard him, when he fails in his trust? If this be reasonable in particular cases of private men, why should it be otherwise in that of the greatest moment, where the welfare of millions is concerned, and also where the evil, if not prevented, is greater, and the redress very difficult, dear, and dangerous?

§ 241. But farther, this question, ("Who shall be judge?") cannot mean, that there is no judge at all: for where there is no judicature on earth, to decide controversies among men, God in heaven is judge. He alone, it is true, is judge of the right. But every man is judge for himself, as in all other cases, so in this, whether another has put himself into a state of war with him, and whether he should appeal to the Supreme Judge, as Jephtha did.

§ 242. If a controversy arise betwixt a prince and some of the people, in a matter where the law is silent, or doubtful, and the thing be of great consequence, I should think the proper umpire, in such a case, should be the body of the people: for in cases where the prince has a trust reposed in him, and is dispensed from[7] the common ordinary rules of the law; there, if any men find themselves aggrieved, and think the prince acts contrary to, or beyond that trust, who so proper to judge as the body of the people, (who, at first, lodged that trust in him) how far

---

1 *broaching* Bringing up a difficult matter.
2 *redeemed* Set free.
3 *Egyptian under-task-masters* Locke metaphorically refers to the slave-drivers under whom the Israelites labored while in captivity in Egypt.
4 *resolved* Transformed.
5 *like* Likely.
6 *made* Asked.
7 *dispensed from* Released from, not covered by.

they meant it should extend? But if the prince, or whoever they be in the administration, decline that way of determination, the appeal then lies nowhere but to heaven; force between either persons, who have no known superior on earth, or which permits no appeal to a judge on earth, being properly a state of war, wherein the appeal lies only to heaven; and in that state the injured party must judge for himself, when he will think fit to make use of that appeal, and put himself upon it.

§ 243. To conclude, The power that every individual gave the society, when he entered into it, can never revert to the individuals again, as long as the society lasts, but will always remain in the community; because without this there can be no community, no commonwealth, which is contrary to the original agreement: so also when the society has placed the legislative in any assembly of men, to continue in them and their successors, with direction and authority for providing such successors, the legislative can never revert to the people while that government lasts; because having provided a legislative with power to continue forever, they have given up their political power to the legislative, and cannot resume it. But if they have set limits to the duration of their legislative, and made this supreme power in any person, or assembly, only temporary; or else, when by the miscarriages of those in authority, it is forfeited; upon the forfeiture, or at the determination of the time set, it reverts to the society, and the people have a right to act as supreme, and continue the legislative in themselves; or erect a new form, or under the old form place it in new hands, as they think good.

Index

From the Publisher

A name never says it all, but the word "Broadview" expresses a good deal of the philosophy behind our company. We are open to a broad range of academic approaches and political viewpoints. We pay attention to the broad impact book publishing and book printing has in the wider world; for some years now we have used 100% recycled paper for most titles. Our publishing program is internationally oriented and broad-ranging. Our individual titles often appeal to a broad readership too; many are of interest as much to general readers as to academics and students.

Founded in 1985, Broadview remains a fully independent company owned by its shareholders—not an imprint or subsidiary of a larger multinational.

For the most accurate information on our books (including information on pricing, editions, and formats) please visit our website at www.broadviewpress.com. Our print books and ebooks are also available for sale on our site.

broadview press
www.broadviewpress.com

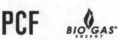